THE DESCENT OF MAN

'With its non-macho slender girth and personal, engaging approach, *The Descent of Man* is a breeze of a read, one that makes you see our male-manufactured world a little differently'
Matt Haig, *Observer*

'A true original . . . one of the most acute social observers of our time'
Ekow Eshun

'What a lovely man Grayson Perry is'
Literary Review

'One of the most amiable dissectors of our prejudices, fashions and foibles . . . a wonderfully incisive social commentator'
Independent

'Engaging and charismatic, quirky and contrarian yet laced with a winning measure of self-doubt'
Clive Davis, *The Times*

'Who better to investigate the traditional male than Grayson Perry . . . both a memoir and a manifesto'
Helen Davies, *Sunday Times*

'Grayson Perry has started a national conversation about masculinity'
BBC Radio 4

ABOUT THE AUTHOR

Grayson Perry is a man. He is also an award-winning artist, a
Bafta-winning TV presenter, a Reith Lecturer and a bestselling
author with traditional masculine traits like a desire to always
be right and to overtake all other cyclists when going up big
hills.

THE DESCENT
OF MAN

GRAYSON PERRY

PENGUIN BOOKS

PENGUIN BOOKS

UK | USA | Canada | Ireland | Australia
India | New Zealand | South Africa

Penguin Books is part of the Penguin Random House group of companies
whose addresses can be found at global.penguinrandomhouse.com.

First published by Allen Lane 2016
Published in Penguin Books 2017
005

Text and images copyright © Grayson Perry, 2016

The moral right of the author has been asserted

Set in 12.02/14.3 pt Garamond MT Std
Typeset by Jouve (UK) Milton Keynes
Printed in Great Britain by Clays Ltd, St Ives plc

A CIP catalogue record for this book is available from the British Library

ISBN: 978–0–141–98174–1

www.greenpenguin.co.uk

Dedicated to Alan Measles and all his
fellows inside every man.

'The truth will set you free. But first it will piss you off'

Gloria Steinem

CONTENTS

IF IT AIN'T BROKE,
DON'T FIX IT

I AM RIDING MY MOUNTAIN BIKE THROUGH THE forest up a long steep track. Halfway up I see a young boy, maybe nine or ten years old. He is struggling; this track is a tough challenge for anyone not used to mountain biking, let alone a kid on a new bicycle. He can't work the gears, and wobbles and grinds to a halt. Tears run down his face. 'Dad, Dad!' he yells, sobbing. He is crying for help, but he is also in a boiling rage. I offer to help him, but he is so angry, so ashamed, that he doesn't acknowledge me. As I pedal past up the hill, I see the father in the distance. He is standing silently next to his mountain bike, arms folded across his chest, staring at his son two hundred metres down the hill. He also looks angry. I have seen that father's face on a thousand football touchlines, outside a thousand school gates. It's a face that says, 'Toughen up, don't whine, be a man!' It's the face of someone who hands down the rage and pain of what it is to be a man. I feel incensed on the boy's behalf. I can't help myself: I say to the father, 'I hope your son can afford a good psychotherapist when he grows up.' The father doesn't respond.

I hope that in picking up this book you have already acknowledged that masculinity needs to be questioned, that gender inequality is a huge issue for all of us and that the world would be a better place without it. What I hope this small book might do is bring awareness of masculinity to more people – awareness being a step towards change, because many forms of masculinity can be very destructive. If this is the first book you have bought about gender, I am joyful. We need to examine masculinity, not just to prevent small boys from crying with rage at their impassive fathers on a mountain-bike ride, but to change the whole world for the better.

Examining masculinity can seem like a luxury problem, a pastime for a wealthy, well-educated, peaceful society, but I would argue the opposite: the poorer, the more undeveloped, the more uneducated a society is, the more masculinity needs realigning with the modern world, because masculinity is probably holding back that society. All over the globe, crimes are committed, wars are started, women are being held back, and economies are disastrously distorted by men, because of their outdated version of masculinity.

We need to get a philosophical fingernail under the edge of the firmly stuck-down masculinity sticker, so we can get hold of it and rip it off. Beneath the sticker, men are naked and vulnerable – human even. It is a newsroom cliché that masculinity is always somehow 'in crisis', under threat from pollutants such as shifting gender roles, but to me many aspects of masculinity seem such a blight on society that to say it is 'in crisis' is like saying racism was 'in crisis' in civil-rights-era America. Masculinity needs to change. Some may question this, but they are often white middle-class men with nice jobs and nice families: the current state of masculinity is biased in their favour. What about all the teenagers who think the only manly way out of poverty and dysfunction is to become a criminal? What about all the lonely men who can't get a partner, have trouble making friends and end up killing themselves? What about all the angry men who inflict their masculine baggage on the rest of us? All of us males need to look at ourselves with a clear eye and ask what sort of men would make the world a better place, for everyone.

When we think about masculinity and men, the issues can quickly become scarily global and serious. A discussion about hipster fashions or who does the washing-up can rapidly spiral into a debate about rape, war, terrorism, religious oppression and predatory capitalism. I sometimes watch the evening news on television and think all the world's problems can be boiled down to one thing: the behaviour of people with a Y chromosome. Men seem to be the ones with the power, the money, the guns and the criminal records. The consequences of rogue masculinity are, I think, one of the biggest issues, if not the biggest issue, facing the world today. Some forms of masculinity – particularly if starkly brutal or covertly domineering – are toxic to an equal, free and tolerant society.

Understandably, women have led the discussion about gender. They are the ones who have been most oppressed by its constraints, after all. On the subject of gender, the feelings of many men can be summed up as 'if it ain't broke, don't fix it'; the status quo seems to work for them. But I am asking, 'Does it? Really?' What if half the victims of masculinity are men? Masculinity might be a straitjacket that is keeping men from 'being themselves', whatever that might mean. In their drive for domination, men may have neglected to prioritize vital aspects of being wholly human, particularly issues around mental health. In their drive to be successfully masculine, men may be preventing their greater self from being successfully happy. I want to unpack what the American feminist Peggy McIntosh calls the 'invisible weightless knapsack' of male privilege, full of 'special provisions, maps, passports, codebooks, visas, clothes, tools, and blank checks', to see if it is as much a burden to some men as a boon.

I feel I need to say here that in no way am I setting myself against men in general, not least because I am one. Nor am I against all masculinity: I can be as masculine as the next guy. This book is about what I think masculinity is, and questioning whether masculinity is working for us, making us happy. One of the problems when talking about masculinity is the confusion between sex (male) and gender (man). The physical, definite, pretty much unchanging fact of the male body can make us think that all the behaviours, feelings and culture associated with that body (masculinity) are also immutably writ in flesh. For many males, being masculine, acting in a manly way, is as unquestionably a biological part of them as their penis and testicles and deep voice. But masculinity is mainly a set of habits, traditions and beliefs historically associated with being a man. Our bodies take tens of millennia to evolve even slightly, but behaviours seen as masculine can be as transient as a teenage fad, a coalmine or a forgotten deity. We need to shift away from seeing masculinity as a closed set of behaviours and from seeing change as threatening, unnatural and feminizing. I see masculinity as being how men behave at present. I think it needs to change to include behaviours that are at present regarded by many as feminine, behaviours that are sensible, life-enhancing and planet-saving.

I can't remember the first time I realized I was male, I doubt many men can, but that is at the nub of masculinity; it is there at the very basement level of our identity. Before we learn to speak or understand language, we are being indoctrinated in gender. The first question most people ask when they hear of a birth is 'Is it a boy or a girl?' Once we know the sex of a baby, we often coo over it in gendered ways: 'Isn't she beautiful?' 'Look at him kick, he's going to be a footballer.' Before they can spell their own names children are well versed in the potent clichés of gender; girls play fairy dolls, make-up and gossip and a boy's world is full of spaceships, action and competition.

So masculinity is a deeply woven component of the male psyche. But I am a transvestite; I am turned on by dressing up in clothes that are heavily associated with being female. This is perhaps some unconscious renunciation of being a man, or at least a fantasy flight towards femininity. I sometimes like to pretend I am a woman, so from a young age I have felt that masculinity was optional for someone with a penis. Because I am a transvestite, people often assume that this gives me a special insight into the opposite gender. But this is rubbish: how can I, brought up as a man, know anything about the experience of being a woman? It would be insulting to women if I thought I did. If anything, it gives me a sharper insight into what it is to be a man, since from the age of twelve I have been intensely questioning my own masculinity. I have had to step slightly outside myself, a doubter at the gates of the crumbling superdome of masculinity. This does not mean that I have stepped into femininity, but it is no surprise that I am thoroughly fascinated by masculinity, the lumbering beast within me which I have tried to suppress and negotiate with my entire life.

As a twelve-year-old rummaging in my mother's wardrobe, I felt dangerously weird and alone. I didn't even know that such a thing as transvestism existed or that other men felt the same. This feeling prompted the thought that masculinity is an act played out blindly by many men who have had no reason or impulse to question what it is they are doing. One thing I discovered in investigating the nature of identity for my TV series and exhibition *Who Are You?* was that identity is an ongoing performance, not a static state. The philosopher Julian Baggini wrote that '"I" is a verb masquerading as a noun.'

I can't remember a time when I embraced being a man fully, unquestioningly. I am a white man, a rather tarnished badge to wear these days, weighted with guilt and shame at the behaviour of one's fellows. Manliness for my young self was problematic. Somewhere there was always a nagging suspicion that masculinity was inherently wrong and needed to be controlled. My mother used me, her eldest son, as a sounding board to vent all her rage against men. By the age of fifteen, I had taken on board a heap of anti-male propaganda. Even today I often catch myself observing and commenting on men as if I were not one of them. Most men are nice, reasonable fellows. But most violent people, rapists, criminals, killers, tax avoiders, corrupt politicians, planet despoilers, sex abusers and dinner-party bores do tend to be, well . . . men.

I did not have good role models. My father left when I was just four years old, and I didn't really have any meaningful contact with him until I was fifteen, by which time I was pretty well hard-wired with my own version of masculinity and its attendant sexuality, something that I still have forty years later. My stepfather, with whom I lived for the majority of my childhood, was a volatile and violent man of whom I was terrified. So men were unreliable, brutish, distant, and uninterested in me. I have suffered at the hands of individual men and with the constraints of gender itself. I am a male person, and I have learned to have some compassion for myself and hope to have compassion for males in general. I write this book with goodwill and in the hope that men will learn to flourish in a changing world.

This is not about writing men off: one thing that thinking about this book has made me realize is that, despite my gender dysphoria, I can be a very traditionally masculine man. There is a corny saying in therapy circles, 'if you spot it, you've got it', which means that if you notice behaviour in others, it's probably because you behave in the same way. I have been masculinity-spotting for quite a while now, and note I display quite acutely some of the traits we associate with men. I am very competitive and territorial, particularly towards other men. I often ask other men about this and they usually deny bristling at rivals or having any other such man moments, which leaves me feeling like I am a macho monster for admitting to wanting to get one over on other guys in petty ways. Maybe my circumstances, being a transvestite and an artist, mean that I am less invested in society's ideals of masculinity than many men and that therefore I am willing to pick them out and question them, even in myself. I feel I have nothing to lose but some antisocial habits.

When I was growing up, my unconscious dealt with the issue of masculinity in a very particular way: it handed the role over to my teddy bear. Maybe at some level I sensed that being fully the man I could be was dangerous in a house with my stepfather. Overt masculinity on my part might have challenged the Minotaur in my home and provoked his thunderous rage. The glorious workings of the unconscious had a way of dealing with this: I parked my dominant masculine qualities with my best friend Alan Measles, my teddy. Also, given my lack of decent male role models, maybe my unconscious thought it best just to bloody invent one, and a really perfect one at that. One that I think I may still be trying to live up to.

I had been given my teddy for my first Christmas and had really bonded with him by the time I contracted measles at three, hence his surname. His Christian name came from my next-door neighbour's son, Alan, who was my best friend. Ironically, though, it was also my stepfather's middle name, and the name my mother used to address him, so in my head the role of alpha masculinity was a battlefield of the two Alans. Alan Measles featured in all my childhood games – physically at first, hence his well-worn appearance, but, as I grew up, Alan became an imagined character in the rambling, looping narratives of battles and races that I played out with Lego and Airfix models in my bedroom. My unconscious playful imagination allocated Alan the role of benign dictator, and I was given the role of his bodyguard. A strange, unglamorous role for a child's fantasy, you may think, but perhaps vital if we think what freight Alan had unwittingly inherited. To a great extent, Alan Measles had become my masculinity. He represented for me an idealized manhood, and symbolized qualities that in my young life I felt were those of a good man. Alan also had strong connections with the mysterious organization I now call the Department of Masculinity. This is something like the Stasi, an organization that makes sure no one dissents from the dominant man script. Alan was a rebel leader, our territory had been invaded by the Germans (this was only twenty years after the Second

World War), and the Germans were of course my stepfather, so we fought a guerrilla war from a secret valley base (my bedroom) which continued until I was fifteen.

The synaptic artillery of that psychic war still echoes in my head. Recently I saw a picture of a new model of Jaguar car featured in a magazine. It was a red F-Type, all snarling snout and bulging flanks. I have never owned a car, but I felt a strong urge to buy one, a red one. I could afford it, and I fantasized about it ticking as it cooled in the yard of my studio after a furious run around the East Anglian countryside with the top down. I talked to my wife about it; she humoured me. Then the psychic penny dropped. Despite all my achievements, I was still trying to prove myself a man, but in the terms of my stepfather, who drove an E-Type Jaguar. Somewhere in my psyche I wanted to rock up at my mother's house and wave my big shiny roseate metal dick in his face.

Some people might argue that there is no point in discussing masculinity as we can't do anything about the way men and women behave, they are just 'born that way'. Well, I'm happy to believe genetics do play some part in gender, but not much.

Many feminists and advocates of gender equality don't like the idea that biology may play even a small part in gender differences. They believe that male and female brains are exactly alike, that all gender is conditioning, and what's more conditioning by a male-dominated environment (therefore evil). I'm tempted to agree with them: it's certainly healthier if we see gender as conditioned and therefore more fluid.

Even if biology does play some part in gender differences, though, it does not change the arguments for gender equality. It just means we have to watch that those tiny innate biases are not used as an excuse for unfair practices, and ensure that everybody has equal opportunities, even if some groups will want to do some things more than others. We should not deny males the opportunity to nurture and care, just as we should not deny females the opportunity to kill and maim in the name of Western democracy, if they fancy it.

In 1976, social psychologists Robert Brannon and Deborah David outlined four basic components of traditional masculinity, or the male sex role. Number one was 'No Sissy Stuff'. The other three were 'the Big Wheel', which describes men's quest for success and status as well as their need to be looked up to; 'the Sturdy Oak', which describes men's air of toughness, confidence, and self-reliance, especially in a crisis; and 'Give 'Em Hell', which reflects the acceptability of violence, aggression and daring in men's behaviour.

Of course, women also demonstrate these traits, but they are not seen as traditionally feminine. These components or rules of masculinity are strictly enforced: every man senses that his masculinity is under scrutiny and being policed, mainly by other men, just as he checks up on theirs. Every man knows that he has to behave in a certain way, dress in certain clothes, think he has certain rights, and even feel a particular way. But the world is changing, and masculinity needs to change too.

In this book I have focused on four areas of masculinity that I think need examining: power (how men dominate much of our world), performance (how men dress and act the part), violence (how men resort to crime and violence) and emotion (how men feel). This is not a book about sexism, but inevitably, as I am writing about masculinity, I have found it very hard to avoid mentioning the myriad ways that men can be sexist, knowingly or unknowingly. This *is* a book,

I hope, that suggests ways that our definitions of masculinity may expand.

Somewhere in every man's head there is a governor, an unconscious inner voice sending instructions through the intercom. This governor is the boss of every man's personal branch of the Department of Masculinity. This Department wants to maintain standards. Every man's personal governor has picked up instructions from a variety of sources – parents, teachers, friends, films, TV, books – on what it is to be masculine. He takes ideas and images from these sources and assembles them into a model of a perfect man. The governor then sits there, constantly checking that his man is living up to this ideal. If the man fails, he is made to feel unworthy, he may hate himself, he may take it out on others. A man may not be aware of this governor – he may think that he *is* his governor or that men are free to behave how they like – but until he is aware of and understands the Department of Masculinity, he will be totally under its command. I want men to be holding this book when they enter the governor's office. I want them to ask brave questions and look to the future, for we must negotiate a new deal on masculinity.

I
ASKING FISH
ABOUT WATER

PADDLE YOUR CANOE UP THE RIVER THAMES AND YOU
will come round the bend and see a forest of huge totems
jutting into the sky. Great shiny monoliths in various phallic
shapes, they are the wondrous cultural artefacts of a remarkable tribe. We all know someone from this powerful tribe,
but we very rarely, if ever, ascribe their power to the fact that
they have a particular tribal identity.

I think this tribe, a small minority of our native population, needs closer examination. In the UK, its members
probably make up around 10 per cent of the population;
globally, probably less than 1 per cent. In a phrase used more
often in association with operation Yewtree, they are among
us and hide in plain sight. I am interested in them because
they wield most of the power in Britain and the West, yet
they operate under cloaks of polite banality.

They dominate the upper echelons of our society, impos-
ing, unconsciously or otherwise, their values and preferences
on the rest of the population. With their colourful textile phal-
luses hanging round their necks, they make up a huge majority
in government (77 per cent), in boardrooms (79 per cent of

FTSE 100 directors; 92 per cent of executive directors) and in the media (lots).

They are, of course, white, middle-class, heterosexual men, usually middle-aged. And every component of that description has historically played a part in making this tribe a group that punches far, far above its weight. I have struggled to find a name for this identity that will trip off the tongue, or does not clutter the page with unpronounceable acronyms like WMCMAHM. 'The White Blob' was a strong contender, but in the end I opted to call him Default Man. I like the word 'default', for not only does it mean 'the result of not making an active choice', but two of its synonyms are 'failure to pay' and 'evasion', which seem incredibly appropriate, considering the group I wish to talk about.

Today, in politically correct twenty-first-century Britain, you might think things would have changed, but somehow the Great White Male has thrived and continues to colonize the high-status, high-earning, high-power roles. His combination of good education, manners, charm, confidence and sexual attractiveness (or 'money', as I like to call it) means he has a strong grip on the keys to power. Of course, the main reason he has those qualities in the first place is because of *what* he is, not what he has achieved. John Scalzi, in his blog 'Whatever', thought that being a straight white male was like playing the computer game called *Life* with the difficulty setting on 'easy'. If you are a Default Man, you *look* like power.

I must confess that I qualify in many ways to be a Default Man myself, but I feel that by coming from a working-class background and being an artist and a transvestite, I have enough cultural distance from the towers of power to turn around and get a fairly good look at the edifice.

When we talk about identity, it feels natural to

immediately think about someone who stands out against the background, someone unusual, someone distinct. The distinct thing about Default Man is that in many ways he *is* the background.

Somehow his world view, his take on society, now so overlaps with the dominant narrative that we can easily mistake them for each other. We can't unpick his thoughts and feelings from the 'proper, right-thinking' attitudes of our society. It is like in the past when people who spoke in cut-glass, RP, BBC tones would insist they did not have an accent, only northerners and poor people had one of those. We live and breathe in a Default Male world: no wonder he succeeds, for much of our society operates on his terms. Default Man's world view is woven into government, the media and business practices, giving the fabric of society a bias – sometimes obvious, sometimes very subtle – in favour of his sex, race and class. He prioritizes 'rational' goals like profit, efficiency, self-determination and ambition over emotional rewards like social cohesion, quality of life, culture and happiness. Centuries of patriarchy have fashioned the world to reflect and favour the middle-class masculine viewpoint. In order for equality to flourish, Default Man's ideology has to be unpicked from the fabric of society and laid out alongside all the competing viewpoints so that we can more easily weave a just world.

Chris Huhne (sixty-two, attended Westminster School and read PPE at Magdalen, self-destructively heterosexual), the Default Man I talked to for *Who Are You?*, my TV series on identity, pooh-poohed any suggestion when asked if he benefited from membership or if he represented this group. Lone Default Man will never admit to or be fully aware of the tribal advantages of his identity. Default Men are, of course, full subscribers to that glorious capitalist project, they are *individuals*.

This adherence to being individuals is the nub of the matter. Being 'individual' means that if they achieve something good, it is down to their own efforts. I talked to several very successful men who worked in the financial sector, and time and again they would describe themselves as mavericks, individuals who stand out against the herd. They are very aware of the boundaries they break because they are carefree spirits, but they are blissfully unaware of the boundaries that hold everyone else back. They think they got the job because they are brilliant, not because they are a Default Man, and being a Default Man they are therefore presumed more competent by other Default Men. If they do something bad, it is also down to the individual, and not to do with their gender, race or class. If a Default Man commits a crime, it is not because fraud or sexual harassment, say, are endemic in his tribe (coughs), it is because he is a wrong 'un. If a Default Man gets emotional, it is because he is a 'passionate' individual, whereas if he were a woman it would often be blamed on her sex. Default Man doesn't just look and feel neutral, he *is*; he embodies neutrality. But it is a position all the same: Default Men dress to embody neutrality, it is not true that they *are* neutral. If George Osborne had dressed up as a cross between Flashman and the Grim Reaper instead of a business suit when he delivered his budgets, perhaps we would have had a more appropriate vision of who was controlling the nation's finances.

When we talk of identity, we often think of groups such as black Muslim lesbians in wheelchairs. This is because identity only seems to become an issue when it is challenged or under threat. When our identity is working perfectly, we are unaware of it; when we are forced to become uncomfortably aware of our sex, race or class, it often signals bias in the system. Our classic Default Man is rarely under existential threat; consequently, his identity has tended to remain unexamined. He ambles along blithely, never having to stand up for his rights or defend his homeland. What millennia of male power has done is to make a society where we all grow up accepting that a system grossly biased in favour of Default Man is natural, normal and common sense, when it is anything but. The problem is that a lot of men think they are being perfectly reasonable when in fact they are acting unconsciously on their own highly biased agenda.

Default Man feels he is the reference point from which all other values and cultures are judged. He might not be aware of it, but Default Man thinks he is the zero longitude of identities.

He has forged a society very much in his own image, to the point where now much of how other groups think and feel is the same. They take on the attitudes of Default Man because they are the attitudes of our elders, our education, our government, our media. Default Man has had way too much say in the shaping of our internalized ideals. He has shaped the idealized selves we all try to live up to into versions that fit in with his needs. The Department of Masculinity has an office staffed by Default Man in all our heads, constantly sending out unconscious memos. If Default Men approve of something it must be good, and if they disapprove it must be bad, so people end up hating themselves because their internalized Default Man is berating them for being female, gay, black, silly or wild.

It is difficult to tweezer out the Default Man effect on our culture, so ingrained is it after centuries of its rules. A friend was once on a flight from Egypt. As it came in to land at Heathrow, he looked down at the rows of west London mock-Tudor stockbroker-belt houses. Pointing them out, he said to the Egyptian man sitting next to him, 'Oh well, back to boring old England.' The Egyptian replied, 'Ah, but to me this is very exotic.' And he was right. To much of the world the Default Englishman is a funny foreign folk icon in his bowler hat, his Savile Row suit and Hugh Grant accent, living like Reggie Perrin in one of those polite suburban semis. All the same, his tribal costume and rituals have probably clothed and informed the global power elite more than any other culture. Leaders wear his clothes, talk his language and subscribe to some version of his model of how society 'should be'.

Over the centuries, empirical, clear thinking has become branded with the image of Default Men. Not necessarily on purpose, but they were the ones granted the opportunity, the education, the leisure, the power, to put their thoughts out into the world. In people's minds, what do professors look like? What do judges look like? What do leaders look like?

It is going to be a while before the cartoon cliché of a judge is Sonya Sotomayor or that of a leader is Angela Merkel.

The very aesthetic of seriousness has been monopolized by Default Man. Practically every person on the globe who wants to be taken seriously in politics, business and the media dresses up in some way like a Default Man, in a grey, Western, two-piece business suit. It is not referred to as 'power dressing' for nothing. We've all seen those photo ops of world leaders: colour and pattern shriek out as anachronistic. Consequently, many women have adopted this armour of the unremarkable. Angela Merkel, the most powerful woman in the world, wears a predictable, unfussy, feminized version of the male look. Hillary Clinton, in the running for president, adopted a similar style. Some businesswomen call this necessity to tone down their feminine appearance as 'taking on the third gender'.

The most pervasive aspect of the Default Man identity is that it masquerades very efficiently as 'normal' – and 'normal', along with 'natural', is a dangerous word, often at the root of hateful prejudice. 'You and your ways are not normal' is a phrase often blatantly thrown in the face of oppressed minorities. The thinking behind such attacks is behind every decision that shapes the banal, everyday structures of our lives. We need to constantly call attention to these seemingly small injustices, for we may find, like turning off the humming extractor fan, that it seems dramatically more pleasant without the irritations we have become used to. As Sherre Bourg Carter, author of *High-Octane Women*, writes:

> Unlike first generation gender discrimination (intentional acts of bias against women), women in today's workforce, especially those working in traditionally male-dominated fields, are experiencing a much more camouflaged foe – second generation gender biases that are impeding their advancement and adding stress to their lives. According to researchers at the Center for Gender in Organizations (CGO), second generation gender biases are 'work cultures and practices that appear neutral and natural on their face', yet they reflect masculine values and life situations of men who have been dominant in the development of traditional work settings.

Of course, this weird minority, these curiously dominant white males, are anything but normal. 'Normal,' as Carl Jung said, 'is the perfect aspiration of the unsuccessful.' They like to keep their abnormal power low-key: the higher the power, the duller the suit and tie, a Mercedes rather than a Rolls, just another unremarkable old man chatting casually to prime ministers at the wedding of a tabloid editor.

When talking about identity groups, the word 'community' often crops up. The working-class community, the gay community, black people or Muslims are always represented by a (male) 'community leader'. We rarely if ever hear of the white middle-class community. 'Communities' are defined in the eye of Default Man. Community seems to be a euphemism for the vulnerable lower orders. Community is 'other'.

In her essay 'Visual Pleasure and Narrative Cinema', published in 1975, Laura Mulvey coined the term 'the male gaze'. She was writing about how the gaze of the movie camera reflected the heterosexual male viewpoint of the directors (a viewpoint very much still with us, considering that only 7 per cent of the top 250 Hollywood movies in 2015 were directed by a woman, and only 2 per cent of the cinematographers in 2012 were female).

The Default Male gaze does not just dominate cinema, it looks down on society like the Eye of Sauron in *The Lord of the Rings*. Every other identity group is 'othered' by it.

When I was at art college in the late 1970s and early 1980s, one of the slogans the feminists used was 'Objectivity is Male Subjectivity'. This brilliantly encapsulates how male power nestles in our very language, exerting influence at the most fundamental level. Men, especially Default Men, have put forward their biased, highly emotional views as somehow 'rational', more considered, more 'Calm down, dear'. It still seems to be a prevalent attitude that men are the rational ones and women are somehow victims of their own emotions. Under the heading of banter, one respondent in the

Everyday Sexism project reported a colleague referring to 'Lady Logic' as a way of dismissing a woman's opinions or feelings.

However, as Hanna Rosin wrote in 2010 in an article entitled 'The End of Men' in *Atlantic* magazine:

> Over the years, researchers have sometimes exaggerated these differences and described the particular talents of women in crude gender stereotypes: women as more empathetic, as better consensus-seekers and better lateral thinkers; women as bringing a superior moral sensibility to bear on a cutthroat business world. In the '90s, this field of feminist business theory seemed to be forcing the point. But after the latest financial crisis, these ideas have more resonance. Researchers have started looking into the relationship between testosterone and excessive risk, and wondering if groups of men, in some basic hormonal way, spur each other to make reckless decisions. The picture emerging is a mirror image of the traditional gender map: men and markets on the side of the irrational and overemotional, and women on the side of the cool and levelheaded.

Women and 'exotic' minorities have often been framed as 'passionate' or 'emotional', as if they, the Default Men, had this unique ability to somehow look round the side of the most interior lens, the lens that is always distorted by our feelings. Default Man somehow had dispassionate, empirical, objective vision of the world as a birthright, and everyone else was at the mercy of turbulent, uncontrolled feelings. That, of course, explained why the 'others' often held views that were at such odds with their supposedly cool, analytic vision of the world. 'Others', in this case, being sections of society that have developed good emotional intelligence and take their own and other people's feelings seriously. People who care more about people than they do about being right. People who might make a better job of running the world than Default Man.

Default Man has been governing much of our world for a long time. He has done many things well, but it is time for him to relinquish his dominance. I think diversity in power can only make for a better society. Women and minorities bring very different life experiences to bear on their decisions.

Things are changing. Feminist arguments have permeated deeper into popular discourse. The scales are falling off more and more people's eyes. Even men are starting to think the world might be a better place if women had an equal shout.

A revolution is happening. I am loath to use the R word, because bearded young men – and it does tend to be men who resort to such means – usually characterize revolution as sudden and violent. But that is just another unhelpful cliché. I feel revolutions that really effect lasting change happen thoughtfully in peacetime.

A move away from the long dominance of the Default Man is happening, but slowly. Across the world, political correctness is morphing from 'madness' into common sense. Equality must change from feeling disruptive to feeling necessary and comforting. We need to reconfigure what it is to be masculine, so that men can handle an equal society. One could argue that with its impulse to dominate, masculinity is at odds with modernism and its drive towards a fair society. Masculinity might just have an undemocratic streak. Men might need to examine what is going on in the darkest

recesses of their gender and question its relevance to a good modern society. One of the central issues here, and the reason this book is called *The Descent of Man*, is that as women rise to their just level of power, then so shall some men fall. The men who find themselves justifiably passed over or demoted will inevitably feel angry, they will be bearing the brunt of a very necessary corrective. They may rail against women but principally they will be victims of their own unhelpful masculinity and a dominant elite of other men. Power is key. The nature of our leaders in politics, in the boardroom, in the media, in culture, in the classroom, shapes how people think. The face of power is starting to give a better reflection of society, but a good likeness is still a long way off.

Gradually we are seeing women represented more fairly in the media, even if they are not yet always sitting at the right end of the sofa. It is heartening to see a female newsreader talking to a female chief political correspondent about the big stories of the day and to feel this is becoming unremarkable. Such changes in society seem to happen at a pace set by incremental shifts in the animal spirits of the population. I have heard many of the 'rational', i.e. masculine, arguments against quotas and positive discrimination, but I feel it is a necessary fudge to enable just change to happen in the foreseeable future. At the present rate of change, it will take over a hundred years before the UK parliament is 50 per cent female. I'd love to see it in my lifetime.

The outcry against positive discrimination is the wail of someone who is having his privilege taken away. For talented black, female and working-class people to take their just place in the limited seats of power, some of those Default Men are going to have to give up their seats. The trouble is I can't imagine men giving up their seats in power with quite the same grace as they do their seats on the Tube to a pregnant woman. 'I see you are carrying a heavier burden of intelligence and empathy than me. By all means have my seat on the board.' Not that it is usually men who offer up their seats on the Tube.

One can't help wondering whether, for every female denied power in whatever context because of sexism, is there a man somewhere who has been promoted into incompetence? What would happen to all those men in a just society? When people campaign for equality in any powerful group, they rarely dwell on the losers. In most powerful organizations there are a limited number of places, equality will lead to redundancy for those people who are blessed only with their innate 'leadership qualities', being white, being middle class and above all having a penis. We need to work out how we deal with the descent of man, we need to offer some kind of reward to those not succeeding in their drive for dominance.

I feel that at this point in the evolution of our society, discrimination is partially eclipsed by the power of exceptional talent. If an exceptionally talented individual applies for a job or university place, their talent shines out, blinding the bias of the selectors. The applicant's gender, race or class fades into the background and their shining ability takes centre stage. Where discrimination commonly happens is when the panel is confronted by two equally OK, middling candidates. That is when being male, white and middle class comes in very handy. True equality happens when everyone, even the mediocre female, black, working-class ones, has an equal chance of getting the job as their mediocre, white middle-class-male equivalents.

The ridiculousness of objections to quotas becomes clear if you were to suggest that, instead of calling it affirmative action, we adopted a system of proportionate Default Man quotas for government and business. We are wasting talent. After all, women make up a majority of graduates in such relevant fields as law.

The problem for women taking on power is often said to be a lack of confidence, but a study that asked women to rate their performance after taking a maths test showed that they overestimated their score on average by 15 per cent. The real problem is that men overestimated their score by 30 per cent.

About 29 per cent of MPs in the UK parliament are women, a percentage that tallies with the global average, so we are right up there with Pakistan! A representative, diverse parliament is extremely important because its influence will be felt in all sectors of society. The potency of seeing and hearing people who not only represent us but look and sound like us is not to be underestimated. It would stand as a model to all power structures and would be a big step towards making equality the default. Members of a representative parliament would hopefully not vote for policies that unfairly penalize one gender, like the recent austerity cuts did to women. Diversity in power means having an inbuilt devil's advocacy.

Women may be just as capable of being incompetent and corrupt as men, but I believe a 50 per cent female parliament would usher in a whole new culture of leadership, one not centred around noisy, bear-pit politics, but one of consensus, steady debate and empathy. Today, women in the UK may have access to the same formal education as men, but the social and unconscious education they bring to power is very different. We have been governed for too long by a group who confuse their white, middle-class, male view of the world with unbiased clarity. The conflation of the description 'emotional' with 'tearful' needs to be knocked on the head. Every moment of every day is emotional for everyone; we can't turn our feelings off. Because men on the whole are less aware of their feelings, they characterize their often angry, mocking, combative view of the world as dispassionate. The collective emotional intelligence that women could bring into government might actually bring us closer to an idealized, rational sort of power, and away from the kind of bullying, tit-for-tat behaviour we often see at Prime Minister's Questions. PMQs is important as an opportunity for power to be directly confronted but too often it is framed as a macho banter match, a tradition no doubt born out of the bleak emotional landscape of Britain's public schools.

In a gender-equal world, men might well pick up some beneficial habits by osmosis. They might learn that they are hindered both at work and at home by a world view that not only discriminates against others but also inhibits men themselves from having a fulfilling time on the planet. If they saw their conviction and motivations for what they were – their own very subjective emotions – they might take better notice of them and work more effectively and live more happily.

Default Man's days may be numbered; a lot of his habits are seen at best as old-fashioned or quaint and at worst as redundant, dangerous or criminal. He carries a raft of unhelpful habits and attitudes gifted to him from history – adrenaline addiction, snobbery, emotional constipation, a need for certainty, and an overdeveloped sense of entitlement – which have often proved disastrous for

society but can also stop poor Default Man from having a fulfilling life.

I gave a talk on masculinity at the 'Being a Man' festival on the South Bank entitled 'Men, Sit Down for Your Rights!' A jokey title, yes, but one making a serious point that perhaps if men, and Default Men in particular, were to loosen their grip on power there might be some genuine benefits for them. The straitjacket of the Default Man identity is not necessarily one happily donned by all members of the tribe: many struggle with the bad fit of being leader, provider, status hunter, sexual predator, respectable, dignified symbol of straight achievement. High-achieving, sexually promiscuous, furiously ambitious men probably revel in the status quo. Men a bit down the pecking order probably benefit so much from the hierarchy and bias controlled by the top guys that they are happy to keep the patriarchy going. The crumbs that fall from their table are worth it, despite the humiliations of being out-manned. Those men who lose out to or reject the power of the Department of Masculinity, however, and there are a lot of them, have nothing to lose from change. If they see Default Man's power for what it is, they may well find themselves rising up alongside women and minorities, fighting for a future where those who fail in the eyes of the Department can seek success and happiness on their own terms.

I see that retiring the Default Man role may well have an upside for the members of the tribe – apart from giving up the coronary-inducing stress of always being 'right' and in charge; apart from living in a world where people are more equal and therefore less likely to give you shit; apart from the new vast wardrobe options; and even apart from the delicious guilty pleasure of somebody else getting the blame. The real benefit might be that a visible, emotionally aware and engaged No-Longer-Default Man has better relationships – and that's happiness, right?

I have concentrated so far on the power of Default Men who dominate the arenas that control our public life. But masculine power is not the same as institutional power – the government, the military, the law – though it can often be indistinguishable because these institutions have been very male until very recently. The Industrial Revolution cemented masculine dominance. In pre-industrial society, men mainly worked close to home; now men went out to work, and eventually this led to the public realm being more associated with men and masculinity, while the home became the sphere of women and femininity. Some men's rights campaigners have since gone on to blame what they see as the feminizing of men on the fact that women have had to bring up boys on their own for much of the time, while conveniently forgetting that, as with the vast majority of huge changes in society, the Industrial Revolution was driven, conceived and controlled by – you guessed it – men.

I think we can assume masculine power is everywhere; it can reside in every choice, every value judgement, every system, each one tainted to a stronger or lesser degree by gender bias. In 2015 some research hit the headlines that showed air conditioning was sexist because it was nearly always set for male comfort rather than for women, who tend to prefer a warmer environment. Like the fable of the sun and the wind, we may be able to get men out of the power suit not by force, but by setting the air con a little warmer so he takes it off himself.

Masculine power has the whole of history behind it, so it

is hard to separate what is actually an aid to men's power from what is just associated with their power because of that history. Nineteenth-century women's clothing, such as corsets and crinolines, clearly had an element of control about it, but nineteenth-century Gothic revival architecture – was that sexist? It was used by male architects to build male-dominated institutions, it harked back to a time when men were even more dominant and it had overtones of a male-dominated Church, so it could be said to be sexist propaganda, but were the buildings inherently sexist themselves? Buildings like the Houses of Parliament and St Pancras railway station are very decorative and fussy, qualities we might ascribe as feminine. I leave that one to the Gender Studies departments.

The idea that masculine power resides in such things is not ridiculous, though. Even when I am wearing a dress, I use the men's toilets – mainly out of respect for an exclusively female space, but also because there is rarely a queue in the Gents. At social venues there are rarely enough women's toilets. Why is that? Nearly all architects are male.

Up until recently, most designers were male and tended to suffer from self-as-user syndrome; that is, in a typical masculine way they lacked empathy for an average user, especially if she was female. When trying to label acts of misogyny and sexism, there are some easy spots. Builders on scaffolding wolf-whistling; groping on the Tube; not taking girls' education as seriously as boys'; expecting the woman to be the secretary and not the boss: these and many other issues are part of the daily grind of being a woman. But as we ascend the glittering skyscraper of power, the patriarchy – the edifice – disappears into a cloud; it becomes less distinct. Men have been in power for so long, and have built a world that reflects them so accurately, that masculinity is woven into the very fabric of society. I find myself now questioning everything: is that rubbish bin sexist? Are traffic regulations anti-woman? What sort of public housing would female architects design? It has become very difficult to unpick masculinity from common sense, functional design and justice. Men have been able to decide how things are so comprehensively for so long that it becomes difficult to dispute the idea that 'that's just how things are, love'.

Many a supposedly 'neutral' piece of design exhibits a bias towards male priorities and taste. Whenever I wander into a corporate lobby, generally full of black leather and beige marble, and often punctuated by the odd phallic sculpture, I feel as if I am in an oversized bachelor pad. I wouldn't be surprised to see a poster of a Ferrari on the wall and a set of golf clubs in a corner. To give another example of male designers blinkered by their masculine world view: the modernist social housing estates of the 1950s, 1960s and 1970s seemed to put a disastrous emphasis on being 'machines for living' while ignoring many of the basic, messy, social and spatial needs of a community of families, with grim results.

Designers tend to be a bit geeky: we've all struggled with TV remotes or central-heating controls designed by tech geeks who fail to empathize with anyone on a different part of the geekiness spectrum. This is why Apple is so successful: it seems to have designed things for fully rounded human beings rather than Mr Logic.

This does not mean that design or any aspect of life historically dominated by men is inherently bad; it's just that if we are to challenge it, we need to look a lot deeper than gender inequality in institutions. We need to question if there is an unhelpful gender bias in everything. There is no one easy solution. Resistance needs to be woven into every moment, every thought, observation and act. Reflect, observe and bring to awareness male power, then counter as appropriate.

The process of blending masculine ideology with the notion of common sense in people's minds so that it becomes invisible is called 'exnomination' by Roland Barthes. When talking to men about masculinity, I often feel I am trying to talk to fish about water. Men live in a man's world; they are unable to conceive of an alternative. I can't see driverless cars being adopted by a lot of men any time soon, so attached are they to notions of control that many won't even drive a car with automatic gear change. When I talk to a lot of men about a world without the gross bias of the patriarchy, I feel like I'm describing a world without gravity to them, so fundamental is gender bias to their vision of reality.

Maybe one of the most discomfiting aspects of liberationist movements to men – more particularly white men – has been to frame and describe maleness and whiteness. A consequence of the exnomination of white male power has been to see itself as the neutral identity against which all others are measured. Yet feminists and civil rights campaigners made white men visible in ways they had never been before. They started to give the default dominant group equal 'otherness', and white men didn't like it. This feeling of visibility prompted men to adopt a victim status befitting an oppressed group. The patriarchy felt itself wobble and fall a notch nearer equality, but screamed as if it had fallen way below the groups it still oppressed. Men feel they are being hauled in front of the headmistress and given a right good dressing down and it's not fair. Having been unaware of the myriad ways they are privileged, they feel feminism is an attack on their core identity rather than a call for equality. Men's rights groups seem to be rallying points for what psychotherapists would call persecutors from a victim standpoint.

On top of that, men and boys can often feel that gender, sexual politics, prevention of sexual assault and relationships are female topics. The 'invisibility' of the male gender and its dominant subjectivity make it seem to many men that all the problems are with the 'other', which they feel they do not belong to. Because of male privilege, men do not feel motivated to discuss such issues. When I asked what was great about being a man, a member of a men's group said, 'Freedom, the feeling I can just do what I want.' And why would he want to give that up? I can easily imagine a man who is struggling to find success with the twenty-first-century model of masculinity wanting to take it back to the shop and exchange it for a vintage testosterone turbo machismo version as it would be so much more fun. Silvio Berlusconi, in April 2011, said, 'When asked if they would like to have sex with me, 30 per cent of women said, "Yes", while the other 70 per cent replied, "What, again?"'

When modern men are confronted by their list of sexist misdemeanours, it can be shaming for them. Gender equality just seems a lose-lose situation. I think the only way we can get men to participate wholeheartedly in change is to frame it sympathetically as beneficial for them as well as for wider society. How is the male role corrosive of their happiness? What has the traditional man been losing out on?

Men being men, they are probably unaware of feelings resulting from the constrictions of the male role; if they are aware, then they may suppress them, and if they want to talk about the downsides of the male role, there are few arenas where they might feel comfortable discussing them. And the very people who really need to discuss them, those dictators, tycoons, oligarchs, tyrants, bullies and warlords, often in traditional societies, who might go on to inflict the violent excesses of their entrenched antique masculinity, are they going to sit down and thrash out how they might shrug off the planet-destroying privileges of being male? 'Hey, I really think this shooting and looting business is having a disproportionate negative effect on women. We should do an impact study and maybe wind back the raping/enslavement side of the enterprise. This rigid tyranny I'm dishing out is a reflection of how hard I am on myself, you know. It's tough.' No.

Men have a constant unconscious reminder of their inherited power. David Buchbinder, author of *Studying Men and Masculinities*, talks of the penis being like a lottery ticket with the possibility of maybe winning big. To have a penis is to have the possibility of power; it also suggests that if you don't win the jackpot, there could be millions of lesser prizes. The truth is that few men win big: we are sold a dream, but the big rewards of masculinity go to a privileged few. A lot of men are sold the narrative of male domination, but lead lives of frustration and servitude. No wonder they get angry.

Men from lower socioeconomic groups usually denied power in a wider political or cultural sense do seem to have a tendency to find power in cruder, more physical ways. Muscles, volume, violence, conspicuous public consumption. Having a penis can be like having an illusory prize dangled in front of you. It symbolizes a historical birthright to power, respect and pride. Men denied the promised reward for masculinity, and who feel powerless, can coerce respect from those they see as lower down the pecking order, they being men who fail to meet certain masculine standards, men who fall outside their norms and, of course, women.

Most men, clearly, are not thugs acting out violent fantasies, and even the thugs pass as civilized most of the time, but the need to play out some kind of dominance does leak out. In every walk of life, men have what I call the 'dogs sniffing arses conversation', a kind of conversational Top Trumps. A thirty-year-old man at a lower-middle-class wedding might ask what car their companion is driving; artists might ask, 'Where are you showing at the moment?'; cyclists who meet on the road might just enquire, 'Come far?' In those questions there is a challenge: how successful or rich are you? How serious are you? How fit are you?

During conversations with men, I have often become conscious of point-scoring. At the basement level, it is boys arguing over whose dad has the best job/car, or seventeen-year-olds bragging about the motorcycles he has ridden, theme parks visited, computer games mastered. But at every level of education and income there is a version of this. A recent triathlon time might be dropped into the conversation, or the price of some luxury mentioned for no good reason. An arts academic might make a reference to an obscure artist or work, as a kind of cultural slap. Conversation can resemble games of cards, with every man hoping he holds the trumps so he can bang them down and have 'the last word'.

Educated, nice, intelligent, well-mannered, politically correct men will argue that they never behave in such a way, but men as a breed are not over-endowed with self-awareness, and these point-scoring behaviours can be very subtle: their favourite coffee bar is most definitely the best; they have seen the original (of course better) foreign-language version of the film you are praising; and for God's sake don't criticize their toddler for rearranging your record collection all over the floor – their laissez-faire child-rearing philosophy is welded to the top step of the podium in the Great Dad Olympics. Instead of arm wrestling, it's how much do you know, how fashionable are you and how up with the zeitgeist are you? Has your dining companion just spent the entire meal showing you his work on an iPad, has he been constantly name-dropping? The need to dominate, to impress, so central to masculinity, will find a way of expressing itself.

Often these slaps or cuffs are delivered unconsciously. I was leaving a dinner, and the woman I had been seated next to introduced me to her husband. 'Ah yes,' he said, 'I've seen you struggling up Percy Circus on your bike.' I smiled, but the word 'struggling' had stung my pride bang on target. Whether he knew it or not, cycling is the area in which I most take pride. I am very fit, and a strong cyclist. If I am climbing a hill and I see another cyclist further up, I *have* to overtake them before the top. As I catch them up, I will hang back for a few moments to catch my breath so that I can give them a cheery greeting as I pass with nary a hint of breathlessness. I joke with my middle-aged cycling friends that we should all have our ages pinned to our backs to rub in the humiliation when we pass much younger riders. I certainly would not have been 'struggling' up Percy Circus (a real street, not a sex show). He was either projecting how he would struggle on to me or it was a spontaneous put-down. I immediately projected all sorts of characteristics on to his aquiline good looks: arrogant but weak, a cad, smug, probably wears cowboy boots, white shirts and a tan; a typical take-it-all-for-granted upper-middle-class wanker. Not that I, working-class bohemian sissy that I am, have any kind of chip on my shoulder.

When I am outside my own arena of power – the art world and some parts of the media – I feel subtly naked. When no one knows who I am, I can catch myself sneering at other men's forms of power: my power is bigger/cleverer/rarer/more sophisticated than yours! They only have ape-like muscles, a cartoon car, business cunning, slimy political nous, while I am watching them, ridiculing them. I make myself feel strong.

Has modern man always been in crisis because his 'instinct' to feel superior is at odds with the central concept of the modern world post-Enlightenment, that we humans are all equal? It's a toughie.

This irony sits at the heart of masculinity's instability, in that the modern project of equality, technological advance and human rights is also a perfectly targeted attack on the ancient physical dominance of the male body. The brain, the very organ that has given the human race its success, may have long ago set in train a process – modernity and democracy – that may be incompatible with traditional masculinity. Male dominance, and its ensuing culture, was born in an ancient age when physical strength could trump any amount of wisdom, sensitivity and intelligence. The evolutionary result of men being bigger and stronger still finds expression, even in our age of computers, automated factories and robot warfare. I think we are entering an age when, for the good of the planet, we might have to work against the results of hundreds of millennia of evolution. We need to breed smaller, more sensitive men. Get Gareth Malone to a sperm bank now!

I reiterate: men will only come on board when they feel there is something to gain from change. A just balancing of power will feel different to different people: to some it is fairness; to others it will feel like a deprivation. Society needs to put a consoling arm around men's shoulders and say, 'Look, I know it's been tough, and you have done a great job of dominating, defending and providing with your big strong male body, but things are changing. We still love you, but we don't need so much of that any more and you can enjoy other things now.' My fear is that this suggestion will go down about as well as if I suggested to a football fan that he take up knitting instead. Much of masculinity is outdated, but we can't just chuck it on the scrapheap (tempting though it is). We need creative ways to harness restless male energy.

According to Hanna Rosin, men (in the US) are set to dominate just two of the fifteen job categories projected to grow over the next decade: computer engineering and janitoring. In China in 2015, on average 118 boys were born for every 100 girls. Developing countries are seeing the traditional preference for male children begin to wither. As their economies modernize and flourish, it is becoming apparent that feminine skills are much more economically desirable today. Boys and men need to change, not just for a fair society and their own mental health, but for pure survival in the digital age.

On one side of the debates around the crisis of masculinity there is often a call to reassert a 'natural' embodied masculinity that will last and be relevant for all time. This noble beast is just a Tarzan call away from the contemporary male benighted by modernity, and is ready and waiting to rescue and revive the feminized male masses. We see this vision of masculinity rearing its head on TV programmes fronted by the likes of Bear Grylls or Ray Mears. They teach us how to survive in the wild, how to skin a deer carcass or build a shelter from tree branches. I would like to see them

trying to find an affordable flat to rent in London, or sorting out a decent state school for their children. These are the true survival skills of the twenty-first century.

This preparation for an imaginary apocalypse, a return to self-sufficiency, is nothing new. Men have always had a habit of over-equipping themselves, as if preparing for some extreme situation. It used to be elaborate swords that were never drawn, or stately homes with battlements; now it is a car that will go from 0 to 100mph in five seconds, yet is bone-jarringly uncomfortable and has no room for luggage, or a bicycle that weighs seven kilos and costs £10,000, ridden by a man who could do with losing fifteen kilos from his beer gut. Such purchases signal that this is the kind of guy who encounters life-threatening danger and high-level competition.

I think of driving on the road as the last Serengeti. It is an arena where modern men play out the dregs of their evolutionary instincts: pride; the desire to defend their territory; the thrill of the hunt. The nature of cars means that very rarely are we able to look other drivers in the eye. We can't read their real intent. If a car cuts us up, we project our anger on to their motivation. Angry men project angry intent on to other drivers, and a territorial battle ensues that may end with a slightly assertive holding of one's line, a honk of the horn or a full-blown fist fight.

The idea that masculinity is in crisis is nothing new. History throws up many moments when the accepted vision of what it was to be a man was questioned and adapted. The mass occurrence of 'shell shock' during the First World War forced mental health professionals to reappraise the idea that men were born with a natural emotional resilience. Before that came the fear that white men were being physically emasculated by the rise of machines and the Industrial Revolution, only for the working man two hundred years later to feel emasculated by the decline in those same industries. Even earlier, in the late seventeenth century, ideas of masculinity took a knock from civil war, growing capitalism and colonialism and nascent female emancipation. Since the male role is a set of conditioned feelings and behaviours, it should be no surprise that its defining characteristics and boundaries have always been shifting. One constant, perhaps, is that ideas of masculinity have usually run counter to social and technological progress in civilization. Masculinity seems bound to nostalgia – more of which later.

So where are men going, and where should they be going? Many men I know would describe themselves as feminists – though in my macho cynicism I sometimes think that feminism, like any political thought, offers men another chance to be right about everything, especially tempting if it involves putting down other men. Men like the idea of being thought of as leaders, but that might just be what women least need right now. If a man wants to be feminist, the journalist Helen Lewis wrote in the *Guardian*, it's easy: just pick up a mop.

2
THE DEPARTMENT OF MASCULINITY

JANITORS MAY BE ONE OF THE GROWTH SECTORS FOR male employment in the twenty-first century, but I doubt many men wielding a mop would feel they were performing a traditional masculine role. Janitor is not a classic position for a dominant man. In his quest for power, a central concern for a man is that he looks and acts the part. One of the fundamental ideas around gender is that we perform it. Many people might struggle with this idea, saying, 'Gender feels as natural as breathing. How could it be learned? Performance implies the role is optional, not fixed.' But masculinity and femininity are not primarily biological, they are mainly life-long social routines we are schooled in from birth. Our genes and hormones probably predispose us to react to environmental conditioning in certain ways, and so part of being masculine or feminine is innate, but most of what we think of as gender I believe is learned. By the time we are adults, most of us are consummate performers, passing as men or women effortlessly. So ingrained and habitual are these performances that it takes more effort to examine, question and revise them than to carry on strutting the boards with our perfect renditions of 'men' and 'women'.

Not only do we perform these roles in life's drama, but we also have a script. Our most basic, most ancient cultural form is the narrative. Stories affect us at the deepest level. We all hold a stock of myths, legends, folk tales, gossip and epic dramas within us. Many of them we have absorbed into our unconscious. They form scripts that we play out daily; they give our lives meaning. Why do I go to work? What does a good partner do? What do I need to do to gain respect in my community? What makes a good man? So we go through life looking for things that will add character and depth to our role as we play out our unconscious script.

The anthropologist Kate Fox showed me a pyramid-shaped diagram which illustrated the make-up of British identity. In this diagram the broad, deep, communal influences at the bottom narrow to shallower, more specific influences at the top. It starts with *Homo sapiens*, or being human, and the very next layer up is Sex. If gender is a set of predispositions and conditioning that usually gets foisted upon someone with a particular set of genitals, then it is very deep, for our sex sits in Kate's diagram below Modern Western Culture, National Culture, Social Class, Tribe, Family, Upbringing and Education. All of those things will affect what sort of person we are, of course, but being male or female plays a huge part in what influence those higher layers will have. She showed me the diagram to point out how insignificant our perceived individuality is to our identity. Who we are is so much more to do with being human and being a part of a particular society than it is to do with this feeling of being 'an individual'. Our identity is a nested hierarchy of groups, tribes, geography and history, but gender bubbles up from the deep, percolating through them all.

As a child I disliked eating from plates and bowls with patterns on, especially fiddly feminine patterns. I remember being so uncomfortable with the unconscious signals of gender that I couldn't handle my aunt's flowers and rural scenes emerging through the milk as I ate my cereal. I would always opt for blue-and-white striped Cornishware: I 'instinctively' sensed the gendering in her crockery. Stripes are about as decorative as a lot of men are willing to go.

Designers use the phrase 'shrink it and pink it' when 'girlifying' a neutral product. As well as colouring bicycles, trainers or razors sugary pink, they often use another easily read signal of femininity, one that I have become fascinated with. I call it the vestigial swirl. We have all seen one. If you haven't, google 'feminine motif' and one will pop up in the first page or so of images. It always involves an arabesque line, a spiral, a few tendrils and a flower. At its most saccharine, it includes a heart, or a butterfly flitting nearby. The vestigial swirl is a sort of international consumer language for 'feminine'. It crops up on female products like packets of sanitary towels and make-up containers, but more prevalently on unisex items that are being specifically aimed at women, such as motorcycle jackets, cycle helmets and rucksacks. A cluster of curly tendrils even cropped up in the corner of the screen during the most recent royal wedding coverage, signalling to viewers that weddings are predominantly 'women's business'. Curiously, as if to rub it in, these 'girlified' products are often more expensive than the male equivalents, as retailers know women tend to be keener shoppers.

Between the ages of three and five, children start becoming aware that they are a boy or a girl. They pick up in a range of ways that this is important, though they don't understand that it is not fixed. Holding tightly on to their newly acquired gender, they fear that the slightest transgression will rob them of a core element in their identity. So girls fear that if they have their hair cut they will become boys, and boys fear that putting on a dress will turn them into a girl. (If only!) The feminine somehow seems almost physically revolting to young boys. In 2014, nine-year-old US schoolboy Grayson Bruce was being bullied because he carried a My Little Pony backpack. Now I know what you are thinking, with a name like Grayson he was asking for it. But did the staff at the school discipline the bullies? No, they told Grayson to stop bringing in his favourite backpack.

Curiously, material culture seemed much less overtly gendered in the 1960s, when I was growing up, than it is now. Walk into a toy store today (do this), and you will see a remarkably clear demarcation between boys' and girls' toys, one that has become more rigid. The boys' toys are technical, designed for action and fighting. They come in blue, black, silver and, of course, camouflage. Girls' toys are about nurturing, beauty and domesticity, all of course in pink – and not any old pink, but unnatural, Barbie pink. One reason is that marketers know that clear gender signals mean more sales. If a toy is obviously made for a girl, all pink with butterflies and fairies, it is less likely to be handed down to younger male siblings. Fashion historian Jo B. Paoletti suggests another reason for the rise in the gendering of toys: the use of ultrasound scanning during pregnancy. Prospective parents now often find out the sex of their child well before the birth, and therefore they and their friends and family have ample time to go out and buy gendered gifts for the baby.

The fact we now see pink is for girls is a good example of how the cultural expression of gender changes over time. Though there were no strong conventions, until the nineteenth century pink was certainly a very suitable colour for boys. Boys were small men, and men wore red uniforms, hence pink for boys. The journalist Jon Henley wrote in the

Guardian, 'Towards the end of the great war, in June 1918, America's most authoritative women's magazine, the *Ladies' Home Journal* (it still exists), had a few wise words of advice for fretting mothers. "There has been a great diversity of debate on the subject," it wrote, "but the generally accepted rule is pink for the boys, and blue for the girls. The reason is that pink, being a more decided and stronger colour, is more suitable for the boy, while blue, which is more delicate and dainty, is prettier for the girl."'

The transposition of the two colours was gradual, but by the 1940s pink for girls and blue for boys was starting to be established by retailers. A key turning point is thought to have been the 1953 presidential inauguration, when Eisenhower's wife, Mamie, wore a pink gown, establishing pink as a truly ladylike colour. Mamie truly loved pink and would carry paint samples of her favourite tones with her as she followed her husband from base to base in his military career, so she could quickly decorate their new quarters in a way that felt like home. It wasn't until the 1970s, just in time for the strengthening feminist movement to reject it, that pink was firmly established as the girls' colour. The history of pink shows us that the symbols of masculinity and femininity can be totally arbitrary. The props, gestures and script needed to signal an unambiguous gender are not fixed by nature but are temporary social constructs.

As children we instinctively pick up on these design cues. Items for girls are coded with 'decorative' designs, even if that decoration is reduced to a few pink doodles on the deck of her scooter. Those for boys are coded with 'functional' designs; from very early on boys grasp which looks signal masculinity. The packaging of boys' toys is often emblazoned in camouflage, but this military/hunter trope is the male equivalent of the vestigial swirl, and no less decorative. Camouflage offers both graphic interest and a firm establishment of gender role in a universally applicable package. I have seen everything from potty training pants and Babygros to mobile phone covers and male chastity devices decked out in the earthy tones of camo. Young boys who don camo are not all members of the cadet force, like I was as a teenager; they have just plumped for one of the lowest-common-denominator dress codes of masculinity.

Of course, men who *really* want to camouflage themselves when getting up to nefarious activities wear a grey business suit. I think a primary function of their sober attire is not just to look smart, but to be invisible in the same way that burglars often wear hi-vis jackets to pass as unremarkable 'workmen'. The business suit is the uniform of those who do the looking, the appraising. It rebuffs comment by its sheer ubiquity. Many office workers loathe dress-down Fridays because they can no longer hide anonymously behind their suits. They might have to expose something of their messy selves through their 'casual' clothes.

Since clothes are a way of exerting some control on the sort of attention we receive, we invest in looks that are associated with the sort of attention we desire. For many men, the sort of attention they desire is none at all. Boys are rarely praised for how they look; they learn early that they are the ones doing the looking. Often I see couples on their way to an evening function where the woman is dressed in a cocktail frock and heels, as if she is about to totter up a red carpet, while the man has half-heartedly ironed his very ordinary shirt and thrown it on with his second-best jeans and no jacket. It is as if men can hear some distant distorted echo of Beau Brummell, the Regency dandy and arbiter of male dress codes, who said, 'If people turn to look at you on the street, you are not well dressed.'

The strict code of old-school masculinity, where shopping for clothes feels feminizing, is absorbed at a young age. The idea that you can buy the role off the peg assaults the unconsciously held notion that the man is the authentic, natural, uncorrupted one. An erroneous subtext that hovers around gender is that femininity is more applied, more of a show than masculinity. Even the word 'wo-man' has an added syllable. The female wardrobe is seen as one big extraneous addition, all artifice, hairdos, make-up, frills and heels, while men's clothes are entirely necessary for function and little more. Inherent in a lot of old-school male attire is a feeling that it is 'classic', 'appropriate' or 'essential', that it is hardly clothes at all, more like a pelt that grows on to the role. One thing they are definitely not is frivolous or decorative. Old-school men rarely dress for any purpose other than to support their role, whether it be businessman, workman or sportsman. Men can feel that clothing choices are predetermined, that there are no options. I think that for many men, glancing in a mirror to see if their clothes look good would be tantamount to coming out as trans. So I grew up feeling somehow that men just *are*, while women have to work at it. How wrong could I have been?

I have a very early memory of a screaming fit in a department store because I did not want to try on a new coat. Trying on clothes seemed to be all about drawing attention to my body, an appendage I had no wish to be reminded of. I hardly ever looked in a mirror as a child, though how much of this was down to masculinity and how much to ongoing issues of self-loathing, I don't know. I can't remember what clothes I wore as a young boy, but I could do you a pretty good drawing of every dress I have ever put on, so burnt into my system are they. I ended up going to an all-male grammar school, by which time girls and the female had become an 'other' that was tinged with an electric charge. Sex. For me, a nascent transvestite, that charge of the feminine was especially in their clothes. To put on a dress was to don a suit of lights, the forbidden other shocking my skin at every contact point. It could, of course, have been static, as I'm talking about the early 1970s when Crimplene was everywhere.

In forming an erotic attraction to women's clothes, I think a part of what my unconscious was trying to tell me was that I did indeed have a choice. Male clothes were not a pelt that grew on to my back, they were a costume, and if something in me was rejecting the role then it certainly did not like the costume.

When I try to explain the reasons that I think may have led to me becoming a transvestite, people sometimes respond with the question, 'Isn't putting on a dress a rather simplistic way of trying to renounce maleness or adopt femininity? Surely you, Grayson, Reith lecturer, Turner Prize and BAFTA winner, are more subtle and sophisticated than that?' My reply is that, as in all of us, the basic psychological wiring of my sexuality was laid down in childhood, so is it really so surprising that I should use the seemingly childish tactic of cross-dressing? A child's unconscious mind probably works with the same set of basic symbols as its conscious mind, so nice person is mummy, mummy is a woman, and woman is 'person in a dress', like the symbol on the toilet door. One thing I have learned from being a transvestite in modern Britain is that often when dressed as Claire I am the only person in mixed company who is wearing a dress! We used to joke at transvestite gatherings that if a fellow tranny started to regularly wear trousers they were taking the role very seriously and planning on having a sex change, as real women spent most of their time in slacks and only us trannies, dressing as a fantasy of femininity, wear skirts all the time.

The only boys' clothes I wore in childhood that I can recall sharply are uniforms. My secondary-school uniform consisted of black blazer and trousers. First and second years had to wear a blazer with red braid around the lapels. The glowing red braid was a double humiliation, firstly as a sign of being an innocent new pupil, a target for the older boys, and secondly because it was a bit fey, braid round the lapels having overtones of a camp, end-of-the-pier entertainer. Some first years would rub ink and dirt into the braid to give it the patina of a more experienced second year. To compound the humiliation of the braided blazer, my mother bought me a leather satchel in which to carry my books. A satchel said 'child' – she might as well have sent me to school in white ankle socks and Mary Janes. This was the golden age of the branded PVC sports holdall; no self-respecting schoolboy would be seen without a large Adidas, Gola or Puma number. At fourteen I studied every nuance of the style of slightly older boys. Collars in or out, ties fat or thin, baggy trousers short or covering the wedge shoes? I recall watching and aping the older lads' swaggering strut, what Tom Wolfe called the 'Pimp Roll'. I held a constant internal dialogue about how to pass as a man.

As a tranny, 'passing' as a woman is something I have worked very hard on, achieved and rejected. We all work unconsciously or otherwise at passing as our chosen gender; in fact we all work at passing in many ways, whether it's our sexuality, class, race, occupation or nationality. Men are performing for an invisible authority, the Department of

Masculinity. We never know when we are being observed, so we constantly keep watch on ourselves and each other; we guard the boundaries of the role. We are all the authority figure and the prisoner. I often look at men and think that they seem to be victims of this drive to perform their gender. What are they afraid of? Why do they play the man so extremely, whether with muscles or knowledge or wit? I see a giant gym monster waddling alongside his family and he seems to me burdened by that bulging plumage. Who is he signalling to but other men? Somewhere he knows that only men truly have the power to bestow phallic power on another man. Though men might plead that their muscles, big cars and sharp suits are for attracting women, really they are for impressing male rivals. The only validation a man craves for his masculinity is from those who really understand his achievement: other men. Preferably equally high achievers.

The idea that gender is performative and that most of us work at passing as a member of the dominant binary system is unsettling. So habituated is the performance of gender that some people might dispute that we do perform it. They might say that it 'just is'. Though things are changing, many men would still dismiss concerns about their appearance as trivial. To the traditional man, performance might also imply theatrical, which in turn implies camp, which implies gay. Real men in their eyes are authentic, with no need for performance, or in other words a layer of behaviour on top of something else. That something else, of course, is our personhood, our humanity. To imply that gender is a performance carries with it the notion that we have a choice, and that in turn implies that we could change. And maybe we could choose to change in a way that makes us happier and the world a better place. If it is possible to somehow look from a distance and reflect on this situation, it implies that those unwittingly caught up in it could be, well, a bit foolish.

The film *Paris is Burning*, directed by Jennie Livingston, about 1980s drag-ball culture in New York, has a scene where elegant young gay men strut on a catwalk dressed as straight male archetypes, competing on terms of 'realness'. Their success or failure at this task throws into relief the subtle performance all the authentic heterosexual men pull off with ease every day. The men fail because they are deeply infused with camp, and camp, as the window dresser Simon Doonan brilliantly put it, is 'acting "as if"'.

When I talked to a men's group, one thing that everyone, including me, agreed on was that the headline of masculinity was 'No Sissy Stuff' (to use Brannon and David's phrase), or a rejection of the effeminate. This speaks to me of the depth and complexity of men's love/fear relationship to the feminine. When discussing manliness, the elephant in the room was not homophobia but perhaps a fear of *appearing* gay. This fear runs like an electric fence around the territory that is acceptably masculine. This is somewhat ironic, as the Department of Masculinity's long-running propaganda campaign for Traditional Manhood may look a lot like a Village People-themed costume party.

I remember noticing in the 1970s and 1980s that gay men were taking ownership of masculine aesthetics that until then seemed in my eyes unshakeably hetero – construction workers, skinheads, bikers. Now we occasionally see the boundary moving the other way. Foppish flowery shirts, once the preserve of fey hippies, I now associate with aggressive banter as they are often sported by blokey comedians, maybe as a vaguely feminized camouflage to mask their boorishness. I also notice logo-heavy designer man bags

being carried by teenage hoodies. The border between fop and dandy shifts in increments.

Watching a men's haute couture fashion show, one might easily be fooled into thinking that next season all blokes will be wearing calf-length floral culottes and a neon string vest under oversized silver foil parkas. But go to the high street and what's on offer will be a tiny shift in what was available last season, maybe with some slight nod to emerging trends, a 'daring' colour or change in width of lapel or trouser leg. Peter Jones on *Dragons' Den* was once referred to as 'eccentric' for wearing brightly coloured stripy socks. Men are gradually becoming more clothes-conscious, but few stray out of the territory of well-established masculine classics. To wear anything not approved by the Department of Masculinity is to bump into that gay electric fence.

One of the perennial men's fashion headlines is 'Colour is back!' As a lover of strong colours, I rejoice when I can go into a men's clothes shop and buy bright green trousers, electric blue trainers and zingy pink T-shirts. But most of the time the racks are a sea of black, grey, navy and khaki. Bright colour is too demonstrative. We've all seen those photo ops of world leaders: colour and pattern shriek out as anachronistically feminine. The dominance of dark suits can seem like a visual rebuke to those who dress differently in colourful traditional outfits.

A study was made of schoolchildren's coloured crayon use with predictable results. Girls used pretty well all the colours equally, with a bias towards the reds and pinks, while boys on the whole much preferred cooler colours such as black, blue, brown and grey. Some people think there is some genetic basis for this preference. Because the genes for colour vision are on the X chromosome, males are more likely to be colour-blind than females. This could have evolution-ary origins: males hunted, so they needed to see contrast and movement, whereas women gathered, so they needed to spot different coloured berries and plants. This could be tosh.

During my later years at school I was the proud owner of a camouflage army-issue combat jacket, which I teamed with a skinhead haircut. When I came home with my surprise crop, my mother said I looked like I had lice, which was nice. I think I adopted this very masculine uniform as a counter-point to my rebellious sexuality that wanted flowery frills, heels and make-up. Perhaps I sensed one of the attractive qualities of uniforms – that they imply a public role rather than an individual private identity. They distract from the indi-vidual body as object, and I certainly wanted distraction from my body as a teenager.

After the camo came a donkey jacket, the tough work-man's garment with leather shoulder patches, teamed with eighteen-hole Dr Marten boots. I was protecting my softy self with the hooligan armour of the mid 1970s. When I bought my first motorcycle, my mother gave me her old sheepskin jacket to wear while I rode it. I ruined the jacket by attempting to swap the buttons and buttonholes over, so paranoid was I of being seen wearing a woman's jacket. Eventually I was able to afford the ur-raiment, the essential staple of any masculine dressing-up box, a black leather biker jacket. Sid Vicious wanted to be buried in his. Mine never left my back for the first two years at art college.

The leather jacket: whole books have been dedicated to this icon of machismo. Adopted by demobbed American air-men after the Second World War who took up motorcycles to replay the thrills of combat flying, the leather has endured as the garment of speed, danger and (yawn) rebellion. It has

Colour for

red tie

now passed into fashion as a lazy symbol of 'rock youth', or a middle-aged builder's interpretation of 'smart casual'. It hints at a dark side, of risky thrills down twisty back roads. Fnurk.

When he dons a uniform, a man takes on a bit of the power of all men who wear that uniform. When I first donned a leather jacket, I was very aware of the reputation that bikers had. Pubs still had notices outside saying 'No leather jackets'. Bikers were trouble. In Essex there was a mythic violent bike gang called the Coggeshall Bastards who wore plastic macs and wellingtons, which to my adolescent mind signalled that they thought protective leather too soft, too stylish and fey. Whenever I donned my leather jacket and kicked my bike into life, I was taking on an antisocial role. In those days of my immortal youth and before speed cameras, I also tried to live up to it.

These youth cult uniforms seem like an extension of the little boy dressing up as Fireman Sam or Spiderman. I think there is a time when men need to put them away. I still have my original leather bought in 1978 and half a dozen more, but I never wear one unless I'm riding a motorcycle, so tainted has this beloved icon become in my eyes. I am drafting a new bill for the Department of Masculinity. Men shall not wear a leather biker jacket over the age of thirty unless riding a motorcycle. I suppose my irritation at what has happened to the biker jacket is symptomatic of a man's relationship with his clothes. He likes to feel they are imbued unquestionably with his status. Someone wearing a leather should have faced down the dangers of riding a motorcycle at speed and not just been shopping for vintage vinyl.

But, of course, within the macho fraternity of motorcyclists there are bikers and bikers. I was talking to a group of riders at a tea hut in Epping Forest. One guy had been to a country and western bar the night before where actors dressed in boots and Stetsons would stage mock gunfights every so often. 'Ridiculous,' he said, 'grown men running around pretending to be cowboys.' He said this with nary a hint of irony as he stood there in his fringed and concho-laden leather jacket, bandana round his neck, next to his pristine Harley-Davidson. We tittered. 'Real' bikers are judged not by how they look, how shiny their bike is, but by how they ride, surely? Putting a lot of effort into the cos-tume and detail needed to look the part implies an insecurity about his performance of a biker's core masculine values, confronting danger and taking risks. At gatherings one often sees a biker bend down to inspect his or someone else's tyres. What he is looking for is wear near the edges, a sign that the rider had committed to riskier lean angles and speeds in corners. *Real* bikers are nutcases.

Realness, as the men in *Paris is Burning* understood, is the pinnacle of heterosexual masculinity. Realness, authenticity, genuineness, legitimacy: all qualities that back up a man's feeling that masculinity is somehow a baseline from which all other identities are judged or attached. Which in turn implies that other identities, feminine or homosexual, are not real, not authentic, not legitimate. But sorry, guys, real-ness is an act too!

Often the yearning for a *real man* is a yearning for a *real working-class man*. It is no wonder then that men want to dress up as guys who worked themselves to death and didn't whine and maybe even got tastefully worn, grubby and faded in the process. The cowboy hat, buff work boots, Dr Martens, don-key jackets, rigger gloves and, of course, jeans. Blue jeans are perhaps the most ubiquitous carrier of working-man sym-bolism. Presently I struggle with denim. It will be a while before the aroma of Jeremy Clarkson and a host of ageing 'rebels' has dissipated from the artefact.

If jeans signal an almost inaudible echo of the hard labouring man, then the logo T-shirt is a more blatant declaration of tribal status. The brand of motorcycle owned, the marathons run, the surf braved, the successful team supported are there for all to read like a row of medals. Gosh, and there was I thinking this bloke was an insensitive bore when in fact he owns a Triumph Stag.

These status signals extend to stickers on the car, the toolbox, the locker, the laptop. Service-industry drones robbed of a satisfyingly manly role at work may declare their virility through their choice of leisure pursuit. Men will spend a fortune on enthusiasms such as handmade surf-boards, carbon-fibre bicycles, alloy wheels, stereos, fishing rods or golf clubs. These toys will often be ostentatiously stored (displayed) around the home to tell visitors that the man of the house is not just some office clerk, no, he is on the edge, a maverick adventurer. Whenever our man sees or touches his sacred man-board/clubs/bike/rod, a blurry amalgam of all his risky, tough adventures swims up from his unconscious. His starring role in his own personal mythic-man script reassures him that while he works in an insurance office, he has fully qualified for his man licence, issued, of course, by the Department of Masculinity.

Deprived of full engagement with the classic outdoorsy narrative of masculinity, the modern urban man loves to wear anything that hints of olden days derring-do. Epaulettes, heraldic crests and any number of pseudo-functional zips and buckles hint at a battle with other tribes or the elements, rather than a latte and a trip to Topman. Designer Ralph Lauren said, 'I don't design clothes, I design dreams.'

Multiple pockets on waistcoats, bags and trouser legs suggest an imminent urgent need of various manly pieces of equipment – a compass, a pair of pliers, some ammunition. Like a soldier patrolling in Afghanistan rather than Shoreditch High Street on a Friday night. Men are into frippery as much as women, but they cloak it under spurious function. They spend as much, if not more, on non-essential stuff to bolster their gender role. Nearly every masculine garment is coded to associate the wearer with dramatic versions of their gender role. Each extraneous buttonhole, pocket and patch is not really about real function but is as decorative as a lacy frill.

Even genuinely outdoorsy men often camp up their look. Recently I bumped into Richard, a sheep farmer I know. He was wearing a waxed cotton jacket so ripped and worn it barely qualified as a cape. I know he could afford a new jacket, yet he persists with the charade of the weather-battered son of the soil (albeit a slightly posh version). Being a middle-class farmer, Richard wants to imply that he has been in the same place doing the same thing for ever. But despite his life of hard physical toil, I am never going to bump into Richard stripped to the waist.

Anthropologist Kate Fox, in her seminal text *Watching the English*, thinks that the clearest marker of class in men is how much bare flesh they are willing to expose in any given situation. An upper-middle-class man would never be seen in public wearing shorts unless doing sport, and would never be seen with his shirt off unless on the beach or by a pool. My (middle-class) wife said she would rather see me without trousers in the kitchen than bare-chested. A middle-class man might not even roll his shirtsleeves up above his elbow, so coded is flesh. The middle classes, with their high value placed on learning and cerebral ability, can frown at the sight of a male torso. Perhaps it is the association with heavy manual labour; perhaps they see something chaotic and grotesque in the flaunted flesh, the tattoos, the beer gut, as opposed to the buttoned-up middle-class, controlled body.

In the previous chapter I referred often to 'Default Man', who represented the dominance of white middle-class men in powerful sectors of society. Here I introduce a new character – 'Old-School Man' – a shorthand for men who have not questioned traditional ideas of masculinity or adapted to changes in society. The combination of a declining need for physical labour and a more visual-orientated culture, precipitated by the Internet, means that the muscular male body is becoming ornamental. When we think of Old-School Man, he is a self-sufficient provider and a satisfying version of manhood came free with the job. But today many men sit staring at screens and are consumers: men shop for their masculinity. Feminist writer Susan Faludi says that corporate capitalism has hollowed out the social/work arena where men performed and earned their masculinity. Now it has no function in their society. Instead of being a part of a strong collective masculine work culture, men cling on to a version of it through football, or are reduced to individuals just projecting an image. A conversation with the owner of a gym in Sunderland really stuck with me. He says his place has taken over from the shipyard and the working men's club. Men come here to work up a sweat and to socialize. Instead of making iron, they are pumping it.

One reaction to the redundancy of the traditional male role has been the rise of a kind of cosmetic hyper-masculinity. I see it as an overtly performed version of working-class manhood. The shiny muscles, tattoos, loud music and loud cars all hope to pump out the message that he's still a real man despite the collapse of heavy industry and a clearly defined status. These performers pay great attention to detail: hair and beards are groomed in precision lines; torsos are waxed till they resemble figures from computer games. Like a miner's wife obsessively scrubbing the front step, the dishevelment of poverty is kept in check.

When I was a teenager in the 1970s I may have been obsessed about how to dress as a woman but paid scant attention to the aesthetic of my male body. I do not think I was unusual in this as I do not remember one conversation with friends about body image. Boys today are forced to be more body-conscious, driven by the rise in obesity on one side and the unremitting visual bombardment of the Internet on the other. The fact that men are more willing to see themselves as physically desirable, however, is good, as it hints at a change in masculinity. But there is a downside. I think that males growing up today are being exposed to the same set of pressures that results in anorexia and bulimia in females. Today's ideal male body used to be seen only on bodybuilders and professional athletes. The visual model of masculinity now sold to men is as unattainable as the one long peddled to women. One aspect of this sculpted muscular aesthetic is its ease of evaluation. One either has a six-pack or not, big biceps or not. When I was a teenager, the version of this was how wide your baggy trousers were, and how many buttons they had at the waist. Later, it was how many lace holes your Dr Martens had, and what number your skinhead haircut was. Boys love the certainty of these numbers. There is none of the messy creative judgement involved in putting together a bohemian look. If you had the right number, even if it did not suit you, it was good.

An underlying rationale behind the desire for the super-lean muscular body may be that fat equals feminine, sensual and apparently lacking in self-control. A hard body speaks of a clear border between inner and outer worlds. Depilation of the hard body adds to the clarity of this boundary, as well as hinting at youth and classical statues and the photoshopped 'perfection' of advertising. The rise of gyms, factories of cosmetic muscle, is partly down to an increased desire to sculpt an idealized body – a body not formed by experience, but to fulfil a well-marketed visual stereotype.

The muscles may be just for show, but they still take a lot of work and a careful diet to achieve. Not everyone can be bothered. Plastic surgery has become normalized. A woman having a boob job to give her what nature failed to do hardly raises an eyebrow; now men are starting to feel the same consumer pressures as women to achieve an idealized body. Some guys are seeking a 'ripped' physique without the work. At the extreme end, men are resorting to plastic surgery to attain this rigidly defined look, paying for artificial pectoral implants and having their six-packs 'etched' to give them the kind of definition that normally needs an awful lot of weightlifting and maybe a touch of dehydration to achieve.

Hyper-masculinity often seems to be adopted by men with the least real power. The effort required to build huge biceps and pecs could be seen as a pantomime of shovelling, hammering and heaving, activities of the working class. While it is good that men are more willing to take care of their bodies, the desire for superfluous musculature mirrors the decorative functionality of men's clothing. Today's service-industry workers have little need of arms that can bench-press 150 kilos. Male beauty clings to an illusion that it has a role other than looking good.

In body image, like in all issues of aesthetics and taste, social class plays a part. Excess in musculature, like all excess, can easily be seen as vulgar. The really pumped-up male physique could be seen to be trying too hard. The sophisticate wants something subtler. Many ad campaigns for high-end fashion these days feature extremely pretty, androgynous male models like Willy Cartier and Christian Brylle. Sixth-formers at posh schools diet to look moodily thin. Big muscles are not classy.

Though I've yet to meet anyone who will admit to being one, the now ubiquitous hipster male could be seen as a reaction against this shop-bought, gym-wrought masculinity. With his symbolic allegiance to authenticity, beard and bicycle, he says old-school, folky, crafted; he wants handmade, local, traditional produce; he is in touch with nature. I have always been suspicious of the beard revival, particularly its association with prelapsarian, rural self-sufficiency and creativity. Beards are just another easily adopted symbol, along with the Barbour jacket, the Shetland jumper and driving round east London in a Land Rover Defender.

What started as a response to the voracious impact of marketing is now just another set of stock images used to flog stuff all over the world. Men with beards, once anathema, now crop up in just about every commercial, whether advertising mobile phones or mortgages, and the bicycle has become a lowest-common-denominator symbol of fashionable 'quirkiness', hung in cafés or shop windows to show some tissue-thin allegiance to hipster/ecological values. But perhaps behind the beards and geeky specs there is a more profound shift. Digital natives and millennials seem more at ease with gender fluidity. In the last year or two, we have seen high-profile moves towards trans awareness and acceptance. Young men, particularly well-educated, metropolitan guys, seem a lot less afraid of appearing gay. Maybe the Department of Masculinity is losing its grip. Like those once unassailable high-street chains which suddenly go bust, maybe the Department will one day reach a tipping point where no one will buy its wares any more. As with many real stores, maybe the Internet is helping to break the Department's monopoly. Young men are shopping around for alternative visions of the masculine role that fit how they feel. In the future, I hope young men can easily adopt a plurality of masculinities as easily as shopping for a coat.

Our clothes are in part a visual vocabulary that communicates how we wish to be treated, we invest in looks that facilitate the styles of relationships we desire. This has become particularly evident to me, as I regularly cross-dress. When I wear a frilly outfit befitting a little girl, despite obviously being a middle-aged man, I detect a change in the way people look on me and treat me – particularly women, who would often coo, dote and fuss over me even before I was a famous artist. The costume has a narrative and they are unconsciously drawn into it. They often stroke and pluck and primp me in a way they would never do if I were in a business suit.

Actors, when they are preparing for a role, often talk of the clothes as being key. Once they are literally in the character's shoes, they ease into the whole performance. So in the great gender debate, maybe clothes are one of the key drivers of change. All identities are co-created. If you wish to be seen as a powerful man you dress the part and, hey presto, people unconsciously or otherwise start to treat you as one. If we want to transform what men can be, maybe central to their performance will be a costume change.

3

NOSTALGIC MAN

IN THE UK, 45 PER CENT OF WOMEN HAVE EXPERIENCED some form of domestic violence, sexual assault or stalking. Seventy per cent of incidents of domestic violence result in injury (compared with 50 per cent of incidents of acquaintance violence, 48 per cent of stranger violence and 29 per cent of mugging). Domestic violence is estimated to cost victims, services and the state a total of around £23 billion a year.

Several global surveys suggest that half of all women who die from homicide are killed by their current or former husbands or partners.

Gender may be a performance but it is not playing pretend. For many males, being a man involves behaving in ways that have all too real consequences. At its most basic, masculinity seems to be a need for dominance, and the oldest way of asserting it is by force. Men still seem innately capable of violence. But it is one thing to be physically stronger, it is another to use that strength to harm others. Males may have evolved with more muscle and a fondness for risk taking, but I believe most of the harm caused by men is a result of conditioning. Anger and violence are often the only emotions strongly reinforced in boys. A toddler tantrum can be cute, a sign he is a 'strong character'. If a little boy uses force, he is 'just being a boy'; if a boy is being bullied, a father might say, 'Stand up for yourself, hit him back.' For a man to lash out is still so expected as to be commonplace, yet to be a victim of such behaviour is severely traumatizing. The two things are closely linked. A man who grows up in a household with domestic violence is three to four times more likely to grow up to be a violent abuser himself than if he hadn't. Violence begets violence.

I can think of no starker, more damning gender imbalance. Men commit 90 per cent of violent crime. That statistic alone should motivate a government to put gender at the centre of policy, but I'm not hearing it. The cost of male crime to the UK Exchequer runs into tens of billions of pounds every year. What if female taxpayers decided they were fed up of paying for this? If the government can repeal the so-called 'Tampon tax', surely they could ask men to pay for the consequences of the violent chaos – chaos that they almost exclusively cause. Perhaps if it hit them hard financially then men might take the issue of gender more seriously.

When I was a young man, I would act out my anger. I was a world-class road-rager: cut me up on my motorcycle and I'd become a screaming, car-kicking, spitting nightmare. Like Basil Fawlty, I once kicked over and jumped up and down on a motorcycle that refused to start. Frustrated by a call centre, I would hurl the phone against a wall. I once smashed a hole in a fibreglass bath in anger when the shower suddenly turned hot. I never hit anyone, but I probably frightened a few. I still get angry at other road users but rarely have full-on rages nowadays. I have learned to act on irritation, nip anger in the bud, deal it out in more measured portions. Anger is exhausting, toxic; it sits in the blood, poisoning your day. Now I channel anger into my work and I avoid call centres.

Anger is a response to a feeling of powerlessness. My rage blossomed in my twenties: I was poor, life seemed unfair and I'd been bottling it up for a while.

I grew up with a violent man. My stepfather moved in when I was about five years old. He lashed out in temper. He was very physically strong and his hobby was wrestling. He had incandescent rages. He threw furniture, and slammed doors so hard he bent the door handle. He picked us up and threw us.

He came from a line of violent men. His grandfather had hanged himself because he was so ashamed of how badly he had beaten his wife. His father had also handed out many a beating, so my stepfather had learned what it was to be a violent man.

I held that experience of violence in my body for decades. If I found myself walking the streets alone at night, I would find myself weighing up my chances in a fight if attacked, visualizing the moves. I could not countenance losing. Often, if my doorbell rings unexpectedly, I still have a fear that it is my stepfather coming to attack me. Now though, at the age of fifty-six, I feel more at rest, more willing to admit vulnerability. It took a big man with a big spanner who responded to my road rage in kind, and a hell of a lot of psychotherapy, to defuse my explosive temper. We can do two things with deep-seated anger: we can pass it on or pass it back. I did not want to pass mine on to my child, so I raged at my parents. Not to their faces, of course, but with a therapist. I raged until I was a sobbing wreck. I still get angry, but not at ghosts.

Perhaps the most important force in my life that turned me away from anger and violence was art. Tim Robertson, one-time chief executive of the Koestler Trust, which does a lot of work encouraging prisoners to make art and write, says that the arts help the men dismantle the stereotypes and assumptions around masculinity. I personally have worked with the Koestler Trust and have seen a lot of artwork by prisoners. To walk round the trust's headquarters and see thousands of drawings, paintings and sculptures by male offenders is to stroll through their collective unconscious, the innocent yearnings for stability in a landscape, or freedom in a wild animal, or expressions of anger at the unfairness of life. I was very lucky: art was a way out of the trench of my family history and the version of masculinity it prescribed, a particularly evil brew of violence and emotional cowardice. I went to art school, a home for alienated souls.

My mother had an even more volcanic temper than my stepfather and she could also be violent, but on the whole violence is a man thing. On average, two women a week in England and Wales are killed by a violent partner or ex-partner. This constitutes nearly 40 per cent of all female homicide victims.

Violence is not something young men just learn in gangs, or even in school; at a deep level they learn it at home. Governments agonize over housing estates scarred by crime, football hooliganism, city centres blighted by alcohol-fuelled violence. They put in schemes to lessen binge-drinking or fund safe houses for ex-gang members, while all the time little boys learn that violence is a way of solving problems. Every time they are slapped, intimidated or humiliated as a child, every time they see their father throwing his weight around, every time they succeed in getting what they want by force they are learning to be violent. They are not just the perpetrators. Young men are almost twice as likely to be the victims of violence and make up 80 per cent of victims of assaults by strangers. Violence is the chief way that men, particularly young men, lose out from the current version of masculinity.

Men make up 95 per cent of the jail population. They commit about 75 per cent of all crimes, violent and non-violent. Men take more risks. Men who feel stuck with the expectations of their gender – to be strong, to provide – can take to criminal ways to fulfil those roles if denied legitimate opportunities to do so. Boys, often those who grew up without fathers, in chaotic households, who struggled at school, who find themselves unqualified, unemployable on the brink of adulthood, can be swept away by unchannelled masculine energy. Avoiding humiliation can seem a big effort for many men, particularly among those denied access to power. Barred from the acceptable routes to pride, respect and a sense of self-worth – sporting prowess, a good education, a good job, a respected role in the community, for example – many young men will instinctively be attracted to situations that offer a substitute.

When crimes are reported, the causes are invariably said to be the economy, imbalances in society, religious extremism perhaps. Rarely is the main reason talked about – it's just too mundane. The perpetrator was male. Charities like Man Up who work with groups of young offenders report that 'The idea of masculinity can hinder personal development and growth, leading to negative outcomes.' Man Up helps offenders to resist the stereotypes and expectations put on men that can lead to violence. One tutor at HMP Pentonville reports, 'After the first day of the course one prisoner mentioned that "his mask has come off" – [he described] how on the wing you have to keep a mask on and stay defended, but in this group space, that mask came off and he felt able to be himself.'

For many young men today, being a man is to be like one of those Japanese soldiers emerging from the jungle, still fighting after the war was long over. They are conditioned to be something that is no longer needed. Perhaps we should treat those young men in the same way that Japan treated those soldiers. Hiroo Onoda finally surrendered in 1974 after hiding in a Philippine jungle for twenty-nine years after the end of the Second World War. He was crushed, he felt like a terrible fool and had mistakenly killed innocent civilians in that time, but when he returned to Japan he was treated as a hero. To humiliate him further for just doing his duty would have been cruel. Maybe we should see young men who act out the extremes of masculinity in a similar light, and tell them that the war is over, and help them adapt to life in modern society.

Some young men cling on to a cartoon image of masculinity and seek to realize the man as warrior myth, as I myself once did. I devoured all of the James Bond novels, as well as biographies of ace combat pilots like Baron von Richthofen, Douglas Bader, Stanford Tuck, Guy Gibson and Chuck Yeager. The violent and brave war-hero template lay completely unquestioned in my head. It came out of war films and the glow of a 'just' Second World War. I loved guns and tanks and planes. At sixteen I was being interviewed as a prospective candidate for Sandhurst, the Army officer training school. War in my mind was still sanitized, with clear good and evil. The stench of pornographic suffering had not reached my adolescent nostrils. Being a soldier was an outdoor romp in an attractive costume with distant moving targets, not the messy aftermath of a car bomb in a market.

A career in the Army seemed a natural progression for me at that time, as I felt like I was living in a kind of war zone anyway and was constantly in fear. My body was constantly braced, prepared for the shockwaves of an exploding parent. That was my 'normal', the petty brutalities of a dysfunctional family. Circumstances – my talent for art being spotted, girlfriends taking me away from my fantasy war zone and a house move taking me too far away from the school to continue cadets – caused my life to take a different direction.

War and parental violence are not unconnected. A man who grows up thinking that violence is a way to solve problems can unfortunately choose a career path where he is able to inflict that solution on a wider population. Taking this idea to its most extreme, psychologist Alice Miller thought that the brutality of Hitler and the Nazis found a receptive population in 1930s Germany because of how they had been parented. Reared on corporal punishment and blind obedience to their fathers, is it any wonder that the electorate found the ruthlessly authoritarian Nazis strangely familiar?

War fits traditional masculinity like a glove. The drive to war has deep appeal to many people; for many men, it can feel so right that they rarely question it. All the uniforms, the maps, the hardware, the risk, the sense of mission, the righteousness: it is the long-awaited call to finally use all that masculinity. Like a tool lying in a drawer, a sports car in a garage, finally the moment has come to use it for what it was made for. To let it have its head. Masculinity is to chase things and fight things and to fuck. Everything else is a bit of a mismatch. To be tolerable, masculinity has been 'civilized'. Laws, chivalric codes, etiquette and manners have all evolved to keep man's earthy appetites in check. You don't need to strip away thirty thousand years of history to get a glimpse of prehistoric masculinity.

I sensed it was in play with the young men I spoke to in Skelmersdale during the filming of my TV series for Channel 4, *All Man*. I have heard men talk so often of our generation being deprived of the opportunity to step up to the plate and prove their manhood. Us European baby boomers have lived through an unprecedented period of peace. Our fathers and grandfathers were conscripted into seemingly righteous conflicts. As if in answer to some deep-seated call from within, these boys in Skelmersdale had contrived a war to give their masculinity something to do.

We chose Skelmersdale because Lancashire Police offered us good access, but it could have been anywhere with a crime problem. Skem, as locals call it, is a new town built in the 1970s, just north of Liverpool. Like many new towns built after the war, it was conceived (by men, no doubt) with a very unhealthy dose of utopianism. To avoid the growing blight of the motor car, much of it was pedestrianized, with alleyways between the low-rise housing, described by the designers as inspired by an 'Italian hilltop village'. The dream was that workers would be able to walk to work at the industrial estate under the motorway while their kiddies played safe from traffic. It was divided into four large estates, with access to one another and to civic and commercial amenities via a network of footpaths and subways under the wide arterial roads that cut the estates off from one another and also from the outside world. But the good jobs dried up and the architectural Petri dish did the rest.

The south-eastern quarter of Skelmersdale is occupied by the Digmoor estate. The houses, pavements, shops and fences have a patched quality, a make-do-and-mend feel. There are no signs of any major refurbishments having taken place. It's not totally grim, but neither is it loved, at least not by the council. One complaint of those talking about the problem of youth and crime is that there are no parks, nothing for the kids to do, but I saw many open spaces with skate parks and swings, all within walking distance, though probably, of course, on enemy territory. There were boundaries I could not see.

The idealism of the architects and town planners had paradoxically created the perfect environment to facilitate gang warfare. The intersections and alleyways, inaccessible to police patrol cars, provided perfect escape routes and vantage points for drug dealers; the subways provided flashpoints for confrontation and robbery; while the estates, marooned by busy dual carriageways, fostered a sense of postcode identities and their inherent rivalries.

Paul, Kevin, Dean and Co. were white (very white for people who spent so much time outdoors) and about seventeen. 'Gang' is perhaps too formal a term for this loose-knit group of teenagers, who paced and ducked back and forth around the armoured convenience store at the end of Castlehey. They prowled like caged cats, full of restless energy, whether from youth or endless cans of Red Bull energy drink. They wore the uniform of North Face black waterproof jacket and tracksuit trousers, black baseball cap and low-key black or grey trainers. Dressing for CCTV, I might call it.

Their look was comfy and baggy, a disguise in its very neutrality and ubiquity – even their sworn enemies wore the same uniform. Not a showy, body-conscious look, no rippling hard muscles on display. A look for the shadows and for running. I noticed that some of them wore two tops and two pairs of trousers in the June heat. I asked Dean why. 'Just a fashion,' he replied. The real reason, it turned out, was to enable a quick change when sprinting away from the scene of the crime. A rather hot, uncomfortable way, I thought, of implying to your peers that you were always ready for illegal action.

As masculine fashions go, it seemed weirdly infantile and emasculating, like a giant Babygro. One of the police officers I talked to spoke of their 'arrested development', how immature the young men they arrested were. Many had never been as far as Liverpool, let alone abroad. Their world was the estate, and carving a niche in the hierarchy. They seemed like a tribe uncontacted by the outside world: they talked little of culture like TV or the Internet, they were always out mooching, smoking dope, smirking, facing inward. To some extent, they seemed to have lost the ability to relate to others. They mumbled half-finished slang sentences, snickered at private jokes.

On seeing our camera, they pulled their caps down and the collar of their jackets up and mumbled through a slot between them. But these were the last remnants of the group – the previous year's police operation, Nemesis, had swept many of the Digmoor lads off to jail.

These were young men brought up by women. When I asked them about their fathers, they spat out a few insults. Their fathers were absent, long gone, in jail, or high somewhere. Their male role models were their peers, or the slightly older lads, the ones they ran errands for or kept look out for. Some of them had dropped out of school before they had learned to read. In their presence I felt profoundly depressed.

It was as if, stripped of all the opportunities that modern

society offers a young man – through education, achievement, talent, social skills, love – they had resorted to a
prehistoric source of pride and status: territory. Perhaps, for
them, the civilizing effects of culture were so threadbare that
raw evolution poked through in a need to violently defend
the patch of the pack. One lad, who had been arrested for
carrying a knife in his sock, said he patrolled the borders of
the neighbouring estate, Tanhouse, to protect the house and
property of his family. I smelt a basic feeling looking for a
rationale. I suspect he had an unconscious need to defend
something, to feel heroic, and then came up with a semi-
plausible motive.

This need to protect territory runs even deeper in some
cultures. In the remote Romanian province of Maramureş,
men still regularly kill each other over minuscule patches of
land, as little as a hand's breadth. Farms are tiny – half of the
9 million farms in the EU are in Romania. We often hear
about boundary disputes between ordinary suburban neigh-
bours in the UK, too. There have even been murders.

In Skem, the young men unconsciously sniffed out something for their masculinity to do. They guarded their scrap
of moth-eaten grass and a low wall, their base, from which
they had good sight lines to spot the 'feds' or postcode rivals.
They said they did it 'for the buzz', but apart from the very
sporadic excitement of living out some dystopian computer
game, this seemed a very tedious existence.

Speaking to these young men, some in custody, I asked
them how they had ended up in this situation. They cited
bad parenting, poor education, lack of employment opportunities, no leisure facilities – all the usual classic reasons,
and they were right. But when I asked them how come nearly
everyone I spoke to who had been involved in crime around

there was male, they seem stumped. Surely the females grew up with the same parents, the same schools, the same job opportunities? My conclusion was that the main social force they were a victim of was masculinity. It seemed to act like a turbo attached to all the other social forces, and it had driven them into a corner, a graffiti-covered, chipped, litter-strewn corner, where they sat sweating in their hoods, spitting, droopy-eyed.

One of their number was a scary child in a blue Adidas tracksuit, called Kevin. I noticed him hiding something in the bushes, probably some weed or a knife. He insisted that 'nobody tells little Kev what to do', but it rang so tragic-ally hollow. It felt like these young men had never made any choices, they had never developed a sense of agency, they had never had anyone to encourage in them those other very masculine traits: drive, ambition, competitiveness. When parents are unreliable, kids learn to take what they can, when they can. They never develop a sense of delayed gratification. Life just happens to them, they drift with the current, they blame, they act out. Soon after I met him, Kevin committed a serious violent assault and got a lengthy prison sentence. I started to think that one of the real rea-sons these boys had drifted into crime was just that it was the most convenient option.

I'm sure a big part of the appeal of this hermetic micro-culture is that it is *theirs*, not their parents' or society's; they are teenagers doing what teenagers do, separating from their parents. It is also an exciting game: crime offers easy-access thrills for young men with no experience of the joys of hard work and long-term goals. While other boys their age do backflips on their BMX bikes or start a band, they are goading the police or stealing mopeds. It is also a game with real rewards (though I'm always shocked at how little money criminals will risk prison for) and real consequences. They often end up playing this game to the death. We visited the site of a particularly horrific gang murder. The shrine had been cleared but the graffiti tributes were still legible on the wall. In another incident, one angelic-faced lad had narrowly escaped dying the year before, having been set upon by Tanhouse and stabbed a dozen times. I wanted to talk to him about it, but he went mute on us. Was this some Digmoor 'omertà', or just the inarticulacy of young men?

They seemed to be victims of an ancient set of instincts and emotions, a need to protect, to survive in a harsh environment. When you are walled off by poverty, dysfunction and, yes, masculinity from the consolations of society and culture, something prehistoric takes over. These lads were still huddled round a campfire, or defending their arbitrary perimeter. They had an 'us' and a 'them'; drug dealing just seemed like the current rationale to hang them on. Generations of criminality had soaked into them and their bleak patch, their swaggering masculinity a tragic *cri de cœur*. Dealing, threatening, fighting was just what they did. They seemed to have no conception of an alternative; they were locked into a ritualistic playing out of the basest masculinity. They had just the bones of it, any culture, skill, aspiration or discipline having long since boiled away. A bit like Donald Trump really.

They gave lip service to basic notions of honour, saying that they looked out for their mates, that there was strength in the group. But when asked if they visited their associates when they were ill or in prison, this 'loyalty' seemed to fizzle out. Caring beyond the parameters of their macho game – well, maybe that was girls' work.

It needs to be said that these young men are a tiny minority. Decent working-class life goes on all around them, but a few young men like these can blight life for thousands. On encountering this group, I was surprised by my feelings. I found them a hard bunch to feel any kind of affection for. Perhaps it was because at sixteen I was very nearly one of them myself. They too were refugees from chaotic, abusive childhoods. Perhaps I should have felt more compassion. I think I was concentrating on their masculinity, and I was none too keen on their version of it. They brought back old fears in me.

It is naive to assume that violence is going to go away any time soon – to watch the news on TV is to confirm that violence is woven deep into human society. I realize that I am only free and rich enough to pontificate on men and violence because we have legitimized violent gangs – the police and the armed forces – looking after us and patrolling our perimeters. Men who have done very well out of the system – usually white, usually middle class, always middle-aged – send younger men, not that different from those in Skem, to be killed and maimed in order to defend our citizens, our borders, our values. Whenever I see 'our boys' going into battle against some retrograde ideology, I half joke, 'There they go to defend my right to dress in a frilly frock, make rude pottery and take the piss.'

I am a member of a generation who has escaped conscription; war is voluntary in the UK. In debates about what to do about feckless youth, the idea of some kind of conscription often comes up, whether into the military or a type of peace corps. Compulsory military service is seen as a bad thing, partly because the popular narrative of the soldier seems to be that of a traumatized hero. This image of the suffering warrior, sacrificing life, limb and sanity for his country, has dominated the media for a while. But I think the majority of men who have served in the military since the Second World War would say it was a very positive experience that gave them good skills that transferred well to civilian life. Most men find the time that they spent in the armed forces overwhelmingly beneficial. I've talked to wounded veterans and often a big part of their sadness is that they can no longer be soldiers.

I am not going to advocate that the answer to young male crime is bringing back conscription, but national service was the last time we had a formalized coming-of-age ritual for a majority of young men. Many men talk of their time in the military as the making of them: it helped them to leave behind a chaotic childhood, and was a time of re-parenting. 'I'm yer muvver now, son,' says the sergeant major to the private. We do need to find a way of dealing with unsocialized masculine energy.

Another traditional way out of crime is through sport, particularly boxing clubs, as some young men see training as a respectably manly excuse for not going out robbing. Boxing is a way of channelling their anger and disciplining their chaotic lives. Several of the cage fighters I talked to gave similar reasons for getting into MMA. It seems sensible that any scheme set up to deal with youth crime acknowledges that the anger, dysfunction and need for risk are not going to go away. These are not just issues on bleak council estates. I look at the news, and the driving force behind so many of the world's problems seems to be out-of-control masculinity.

I am depressed at how a hopeful Arab Spring turned into a continent-wide conflagration. Maybe I shouldn't be surprised – blokes do love guns. To people like me, ISIS seems like a bonkers death cult, but maybe to teenage boys its slick online propaganda seems to offer a very enticing passage to manhood. A risky, collective boy's own adventure in the name of a seductively black-and-white world view. A chance to play out all those bedroom dreams of anti-establishment heroism for real. ISIS is not breeding killers, it is just appealing to disaffected young men seeking a place where their anger, alienation and ideals of manhood seem to fit.

Traditional masculinity can also present qualities to be exploited in the global pissing contest. Shame and humiliation are big issues for 'traditional' men. Not for nothing did the CIA deliberately humiliate prisoners in Guantanamo Bay with anal penetration, getting them to simulate homosexual acts, taunting by female interrogators, even making them wear nappies.

I asked a men's group what women might not know about men. What came up was just how attracted to risk men are. These were middle-aged, middle-class men in therapy, yet they all had tales to tell of reckless driving, drug taking, sex and violence, and they told them with relish. In all-male company, risk is a shared enthusiasm.

I remember being energized and exhilarated by graphic scenes of violence. As schoolboys we delighted in swapping tales of gore from the previous night's telly. The moment in *The Battle of Britain* when the gunner's goggles fill with blood, and any number of amputations and beheadings in historical dramas, complete with spurting blood and sizzling wounds, were recounted with glee at the bus stop the next morning. But it was not those scenes that nearly drove me into the arms of the military, it was a search for a comforting male role and an escape from my family home.

Brought up on the cartoon role models of masculinity – cowboy, soldier, cop or robber, mod or rocker – it felt to me like everything would only come into focus in a fight; to be a man was to be prepared for violence. I spent my childhood metaphorically collecting, laying out and checking my equipment. I very nearly took the fantasy through the recruiting door into gory reality. If I had joined the Army, I could well have ended up in Northern Ireland, the Falklands or Bosnia. Thankfully I didn't, but I still had a trunkful of angry masculinity lying there with nothing to do. It wasn't until I experienced psychotherapy in my late thirties that I felt I was able to sort through that trunk.

And before all you book-reading, middle-class sissies think that male violence is perpetrated by the 'other' – the poor, the uneducated, the foreign – just ask a divorce lawyer. The chattering classes might think of wife beating as something perpetrated on run-down council estates by shaven-headed tattooed men in vests. They might think that the strictures of polite good manners and emotional repression as practised by their breed means that violence is deemed terribly infra dig. However, a divorce lawyer I spoke to said that domestic violence is just as common among the middle classes, it's just that they don't tend to leave bruises, and there is a lot of controlling, intimidating, bullying, emotional blackmail, such as 'I'll tell your family what an awful mother/mentally ill/alcoholic/slut you are.' A man cornered by his own infidelity, anger or depression is not a pretty sight, no matter what school he went to. As the author Amanda Prowse wrote in an article about middle-class domestic violence in the *Telegraph*, 'In a detached house there is no one to hear you scream.'

A contemporary Western man can easily feel that his

body and a whole raft of his instincts are no longer needed. Society has moved on, machines do the lifting, and most of the fighting is outsourced to specialists. The basic dynamic of masculinity – the need for dominance – appears to be completely out of kilter with the whole modernist project. As we hopefully, haltingly, progress to a more equal, tolerant society, the psychological and physical tools inherited by men seem increasingly redundant.

The male role in developed countries is nearly all performance, a pantomime of masculinity. There is no hunting any more, no war, little heavy physical labour. The 1999 film *Fight Club*, based on the novel by Chuck Palahniuk, deals with this theme. The narrator (Edward Norton) meets super-attractive, masculine Tyler Durden (Brad Pitt), they form a close friendship, and then establish a club where men come to fight and play out their frustrated masculine drives, a club which develops into an anti-materialist, anti-corporate organization. It turns out (spoiler alert) that Tyler is a disassociated part of the narrator's own personality. I found this fascinating, particularly given that as a child I projected my disassociated masculinity on to my teddy bear, Alan Measles. Although, as I've already said, Alan was then a guerrilla warrior fighting the invading Germans, a metaphor for my stepfather, his role has subsequently morphed into a Dalai Lama-like guru, reflecting perhaps my own, less angry self.

Whenever I talk about masculinity, about its behaviours, feelings and aesthetics, it often feels historical. A trait that *Fight Club* and much of the rhetoric around manhood seems to exhibit is nostalgia. Feminism has always been forward-looking. Women's rights will come, a woman's role will change and expand, she is working for a better, a more just future. Women seem to embrace change, not just in society, but in themselves. In order to take up this expanding role she needs to adapt, learn new skills, become more confident. Men, though, always seem to be harking back to some mythical golden age (for men) when men were 'men'. A time of hunting (dangerous, thrilling), a time of war (dangerous, thrilling and boring), a time of heavy industry (dangerous, boring), times when all the vintage man equipment – anger, violence, physical strength – could be put through its paces. A time also when men dominated women.

For many men, progressive feminist arguments can feel like a defeat, a slippery slope to redundancy and humiliation. You are no longer fit for purpose, we don't need lumbering, warmongering animal chasers any more. It used to be that women were characterized as the more base, more earthy, more animal half of humanity, prone to 'passionate' outbursts and 'irrational' behaviour. Now, when I watch the news of terrorism, financial mismanagement, corruption, crime and intolerance, it is men who seem base, uncivilized. It is men who need to look forward and think how they might change.

This backward-looking stance seems woven into much of the talk around masculinity. We should beware of nostalgia: it is a common human trait to find the familiar comforting, but the rewards of expanding the comfort zone need to be celebrated remorselessly. Trying new things does not just mean skydiving or trekking in the jungle, that is, ramped-up versions of everyday man challenges. I mean new as in new behaviours: being more open, being kinder to yourself, letting the mask drop.

As I pointed out earlier, old-school masculinity is increasingly sold to the modern man as a hairy-chested leisure pursuit that can be put on like a crash helmet or a wetsuit at the weekend, something he can harmlessly slough off and leave in the cupboard under the stairs while he carries on normal life as a well-behaved earner/father/lover. The huge popularity today of running marathons, triathlons, Tough Mudder challenges, Munro-bagging or surfing are symptomatic not just of a need to keep fit but of man's desire to give his masculinity something to do. Sport presents men with tests of endurance, strength and hard-won physical skills, exposure to danger and the chance to dominate, a perfect arena where all that manly conditioning makes perfect sense. Of all the men I interviewed for *All Man*, the most relaxed around his masculinity was cage fighter Colin 'Freakshow' Fletcher. Powerfully built, and successful in professional mixed martial arts (the preferred term for cage fighting), Colin talked openly and humorously about his manhood in a way that felt like he had nothing to prove. His fight persona of a horror-show clown and his ridiculous tattoos seemed to mock the regulation machismo often pumped out by fellow fighters. He appeared to be a walking (punching/kicking/strangling) advert for the mental health benefits of sport.

Sport is certainly where I feel most masculine.

My stepfather loved sport, so as a teenager, despite being a gifted natural athlete, I rejected physical competition along with him. When I was sixteen I won a running race at school and he said to me, 'About time you did something with your body instead of your brain.' I never ran in competition again.

It was another sixteen years later that I truly rekindled my relationship with my physical prowess.

In those intervening years I practised the anti-sport of skateboarding. Skateboarding was Californian cool laced with a punk aggression. It was not about endurance or speed, it seemed to be mainly about attitude. I started as that saddest of teens, the rural skateboarder who had to walk a couple of miles to the nearest stretch of rideable tarmac. Skateboarding really came alive for me when I began squatting in central London in 1983. There was a growing cult around the early, free (and on the whole useless) skate spots: Cantelowes Gardens, Kennington Park, the Southbank and, my favourite, Meanwhile 2 under the Westway. Occasionally I would travel out to the Rom, a commercial skate park in Romford (now a listed structure).

We would ride wide, fish-shaped boards with hard wheels, and wear Converse and eye-scorching baggy surf shorts well before they became fashion staples. We read about our West Coast heroes in *Thrasher* magazine, which began as a few stapled-together photocopies sold in the skate shop under Rough Trade records in Notting Hill. The skating crowd was intimidating, urban and, of course, entirely male. The best skaters were not necessarily the ones who could pull off the hardest tricks, they were the guys who had a fully committed daring but with almost balletic machismo. They would be very cool: it was de rigueur to be insouciant about such physical skill. Pulling a good pose while airborne was part of the game; ripped shorts, burst shoes and splintered boards all added style points. The entry fee to an informal competition might be having to drink a can of lager before performing.

This was how I got my adrenaline kicks for a decade or so from 1977, till falling off on to concrete was really starting to hurt too much. I then switched to mountain biking, which seemed relatively safe in comparison. In the 1980s, cycling, apart from BMX riding, was seen as nerdy, the preserve of old northern men on uncomfortable road bikes, eating sand-wiches while leaning against fingerposts. Mountain biking, which really took off in the 1990s, was something different though: playful, tougher, and on the whole more arse- and elbow-friendly. They are still the choice of the hoody who needs to escape the police by crashing up a kerb and slipping down an alley while checking a text.

I was quickly drawn from tootling through Epping Forest into the organized sport, and participated in my first cross-country mountain-bike race in 1992. I clearly remem-ber the immediate visceral thrill of being nakedly competitive (as opposed to my covert rivalries with my fellow artists. Who did the best in that auction? How many people went to see his show?). Passing my first fellow racer, I almost joyfully shouted, 'Eat my dirt, loser!' I also soon learned that skate-boarding hadn't kept me that fit.

Compared to road racing, competitive mountain biking is pretty democratic. The fifth-best rider, barring mishaps, is very likely to finish fifth. Because of the slower speeds and narrow technical courses, there is no wind-shielding peloton, or main pack of riders, to keep up with or gang up against you, so it is mainly you against the course, with the occasional bit of elbowing when fighting for the good line. I raced between the ages of thirty-two and forty-four. Some-one once referred to veteran mountain-bike racing as 'fifty men saying, "After you"!' In truth it could be gloriously competitive. A tactic I often employed when catching up a rider on an uphill section (and, as I've already mentioned, still can't stop myself from doing today) was to hold back for a few moments to catch my breath, then sprint past with a cheery greeting to rub it in. I remember urinating into my shorts, as I did not want to give up my good start position at the front of a fifty-strong grid. I remember slowing down to catch my breath and to hold back rivals through the narrow sections, only to sprint off into the distance as soon as the track opened up.

I soon became obsessed, and the racing gave me a goal to train hard. One year I even took on an online coach to tailor my training. I wanted to find out just how fit and fast I could get, which turned out to be fairly fast. I even won a couple of local races. I was doing four two-to-three-hour sessions a week and would take my heart rate every morning before I got up and put it on a graph. I would bore on about anaerobic thresholds and fartlek. There is a popular idea that artists are not supposed to be sporty, and so this only added to the attraction for me. Like pottery, sport was, well, a bit naff. Racing also gave me an insight into a different subculture: clean-cut men eyeing each other at the start, wondering, 'How lean is he? Should I grid up in front of him? Will he hold me up?' After the race there would be a glorious rush of endorphins; sweaty, dusty men, all high on natural chemicals, comparing notes and battle scars. No one knew me as an artist; I was just the bloke who came fifth.

Sport is uniquely human. It is civilized war, an acceptable arena to bare one's teeth. I dislike sports where judges decide on the winner, like ice dancing or diving. For an artist it is headily refreshing that there is no maybe, just winning or losing.

This clarity in sport between triumph and defeat may be problematic when dealing with masculinity, however. How do you tear boys away from the easy-to-understand cartoon male role and get them to take on board a subtler, nuanced version of masculinity when all their heroes play sport, which is all about clear winners and losers? How do we communicate a flexible version of being a man that is appropriate for

the twenty-first century? Sport is great but life is messy. You can probably write out the goals of feminism on a postcard, but what would I write on the male equivalent? Men like a clearly defined mission statement, but what if the problem is that men like a clearly defined mission statement? What men might need is a set of skills to negotiate the daily challenges of life, big and small, which have no clear winners and losers. Men might need to work less on their biceps and more on their intuition.

If the popular vision of masculinity is in need of updating to suit a world of more nuanced gender roles, who better to instigate this than concerned groups of men. The men's movement has been kicking along since the 1960s. It grew alongside second-wave feminism, the Black Power movement and student activism. It started as a men's liberation movement that looked at how boys and men needed to adapt to a world of gender equality. It looked at the restrictions of the male role, very much in the same way as feminists looked at the female role. Early men's movements campaigned alongside women, but very soon they split into opposing camps who were either pro-feminist or anti-feminist.

While pro-feminism was quietly absorbed into Western liberal thinking, the character of the men's movement changed. As society moved towards equality, those men who were lumbered with outdated attitudes and interpersonal skills started to feel hard done by. These feelings started to coalesce into a different kind of men's movement, one which was openly hostile to feminism. One of the early voices was Warren Farrell, who wrote a book in the 1980s called *The Myth of Male Power*. His thesis was that men are the disposable sex, sent off to fight, rescue others or work in dangerous situations. His book was seen as an astringent corrective to the feminist voices dominating debate around gender. Paul Elam, who cites Farrell as his mentor, runs A Voice for Men, the most popular website of the men's rights movement. Paul seems to be an intelligent, sensitive thinker on masculinity, and much of the site seems thought-provoking and relatively moderate, but I can't help feeling that behind a lot of the writing is a well-polished sense of grievance. Alongside articles on mansplaining, manspreading and circumcision are features entitled 'The Dangers of Modern Feminism', and one singling out a feminist activist that I felt invited trolling. The site has many thoughtful, perceptive things to say, some of it written by women. But I think that the justifiable anger at how traditional working-class men feel left on the scrapheap, or the impossible visions of masculinity that are sold to them, is too easily targeted at women and feminists instead of men in power. The men on this website seem to feel that the thing feminism is attacking – the sexist patriarchy – is the same as their core masculine identity. They seem to talk as if annihilating sexism is annihilating them. On the whole I feel that men are their own worst enemy. What started as a heartfelt call to re-examine and re-imagine a man's place in the modern world has gradually become hijacked by younger, angrier and sometimes openly misogynistic men.

This is probably more down to the nature of the Internet than anything. The Web seems to have the effect of crystallizing diffuse discontent into paranoid, blamey rant fests. Reading posts on websites like Men Going Their Own Way (MGTOW), I start to think that maybe I'm a dupe of some feminist conspiracy and I have been indoctrinated by a misandrist liberal media. Then I think, hang on, I've never felt that hard done by, maybe I'm weird . . .

There are many references on MGTOW to blue or red pills, a nod to the film *The Matrix*, where the hero is offered a choice: take a blue pill and return to acceptance of an illusion of reality, or take the red pill and see the world how it really is. Some of the men posting on MGTOW forums feel that their consciousness of female oppression has been raised, so think of themselves as having swallowed the red pill.

One man, calling himself Silent, wrote this:

What can't you stand anymore since taking the red pill? I've noticed ever since I did take the red pill a lot of things I used to enjoy I don't anymore.
The things I can't stand anymore are:

99% of anime
99% of modern TV shows
ALL modern movies in theaters or on DVD
Public bars
Most online communities
Learning about current politics
Most people
Universities and their public libraries

Places where women gather in groups. (Such as malls, grocery stores, movie theaters, tourist areas)

In reply, a man called Keymaster writes:

I would also add, women can't manipulate me. They lose every time. I find it entertaining and amusing, they hate it . . . but it's their own fault for trying.

It's not the attempted manipulation that I can't stand, it's how arrogant she is assuming that it was supposed to work, and she should just magically get her way.

EXAMPLE #1
I was out on a date, maybe 2½ years ago. Nice evening. Great girl. Then she starts 'Here hold my purse' . . .
'You can put it down over there' (while I just stood there with my hands in my pockets).
She actually looked at me like I just treated her badly. But my inner dialogue said *'if you hold her purse, she won't fuck you tonight'*.

Silent responds:

I've experienced that as well. When I did have female friends, they would also ask me or tell me to do something expecting me to do it. I was a mangina/white knight during those years, so like an idiot, I did it.
Now, whenever a woman expects me to do something for them, I just ignore them. Self entitled bitches can go fuck themselves for all I care. Women expect men to do things for them without them doing anything for the man.
Unless they give me a blowjob or money for my service, there's no way I'm gonna do something for a woman when in most cases, I don't even have to acknowledge their existence.

This is the tone of many posts on the site. Whether these men are like this in real life I don't know, but they feel to me like men who lack the interpersonal skills and education to negotiate the give and take of dating. They are clinging on to an outdated gender role, and resent the way the world has gone on changing without their permission. They talk of sex like it were a currency. These may be perfectly reasonable human beings venting online, but what worries me is that other, even more bitter and alienated young men may read such posts, fuelling resentments that may result in violent action. It is interesting that 'Silent' refers to the 'White Knight' – many women still do buy into the narrative of the heroic rescuer of romantic fiction and have misguided expectations of their men. Maybe instead of 'Going Their Own Way' these men need to learn to reflect, negotiate and adapt with goodwill.

At the darker end of the spectrum is professional sexist Daryush Valizadeh, better known as pick-up artist Roosh V, whose website is called the Return of Kings (sigh). Sample articles include: '5 Ways to Groom an Indian Girl to be a Subservient Wife', subtitled 'How you can turn a lump of coal into a diamond', and 'The Benefits of Machine Gun Versus Sniper Rifle Game: Which one is for you?' ('game' meaning picking up women for sex).

The men's rights movement seems wedded to an inflexible, static vision of masculinity. Women have long focused on what women *can* be, *should* be, *will* be in the future. The problem for women is being shackled to the past, to old sexist roles and stereotypes, while men seem programmed to want to preserve something, some rufty-tufty authentic core idea of masculinity that is, on the whole, no longer needed or wanted. Women have been willing to change. They may well have taken on some of the qualities that were traditionally male. The men's rights movement doesn't seem to encourage men to take on some traditionally female qualities as a counterblast. The manosphere seems to know deep down that their persecutor/victim stance is wrong. The sexist online banter may not be how they really think and talk; they might just be blowing off steam, just beta loser guys licking up to an imaginary boss from the Department of Masculinity. But I worry that, as their ability to laugh at themselves is seemingly in short supply, many men may take all this 'harmless venting' seriously, and it won't help them to live a happy life. They hide behind anonymity. They comfort themselves with paranoid conspiracy theories. They say that the liberal media never covers their side of the story: the false rape allegations, the female violence, the discrimination that men face. Their tone – hyped up, ranting, domineering, aggressive – betrays the truth. Even when they are not explicitly stating what they are campaigning for, it is clear that they are trying to turn the clocks back to a time when real world gender relations matched their sexual fantasies. They have not cottoned on to the fact that to be an attractive man in the twenty-first century you might have to be a bit, well, feminist.

The scorching debate around gender seems to be carried out by activists, the media and academics – middle-class people, in other words; meanwhile, out there is real injustice in both directions.

Divorced from the bigotry-polluting men's rights activists (MRAs, as they're known), what would a true movement for men's rights look like? One that's concerned with ensuring that today's men are teaching the next generation not to distrust or reject the ascendance of women, but to understand it and its importance, to understand what men have been and how they can avoid becoming relics, or dinosaurs caught on the wrong side of history, but instead be truly modern men?

Feminism probably went through this tussle with cultural lag decades ago. I'm sure that in the 1960s, 1970s and 1980s there were many females who rejected feminists as ugly extremists, as bra-burning hairy harridans, but later adopters would subsequently take on board gender equality as natural justice. New behaviours very often seem frightening, then exciting, before becoming comfortably normal. Males need to go through the same process. They need to get over the unsettling 'otherness' of a progressive man and start to see him as the new norm (not the one from *Cheers*). Gender is so deep in our identity that it will take many generations for change to happen. That is no excuse for not working on it now.

But who are the good progressive male role models guiding young men? I'm sure there are many of them, but in public life? Ask a feminist to name five. Obama? David Beckham? The Dalai Lama? Brad Pitt? Erm . . . It's hard to nominate good role models, because we don't *know* what these public figures are like in private. Oscar-winning Mark Rylance seems absolutely delightful, but he is an actor. He might pour hot fat over his wife and lock her in the cellar on his day off. I'm not entirely convinced by the power of celebrity male role models. They are exotic, distant beasts. For the role modelling to work, I think boys need the reliable, constant drip-drip of day-to-day contact and attention from a good man, probably his father. A boy needs to have his mentor's sensibility rub off on him and reinforced frequently and casually, not just read about him on some gossip website or see him on some chat show.

I find few focused examples of what men could or should be in a gender-equal world. I have read a lot about changes in society and how they are benefiting women and shaming men, but the visions for how men might be in the future are thinly sketched. More stay-at-home dads, tick; being less sexist, tick; open up on the feelings, tick. These are all important social changes. The problem is that because they are new there is no compelling back catalogue of the kind of role models and narratives that currently form the powerful propaganda of the old-school man. I can see the need for a new male archetype, but is he sexy and thrilling? He's practical, convenient, like a washing machine. Men need a vision of masculinity that is not just predicated on the thrilling highlights of an outdated romantic narrative – it needs to celebrate the true everyday happiness that comes from stable intimate relationships and a meaningful role in the here and now. I have no unconscious emotion churning away when I think of new man. He seems like a good idea but a tough sell – like trying to sell a car on the strength of how nice it is, when you're stuck in a traffic jam.

But in a way that is exactly what I am selling. Fulfilment of masculinity is often sold on the strength of peak experiences: winning battles, pulling women, pure adrenaline, moments of ecstasy. But life ain't like that. We rarely, if ever, take our car (masculinity) on to a racetrack, so maybe we need a version that works doing the everyday things. We need a masculinity that's easy to park, with a big boot, child seats and low fuel consumption. Men need to learn to equip themselves for peace.

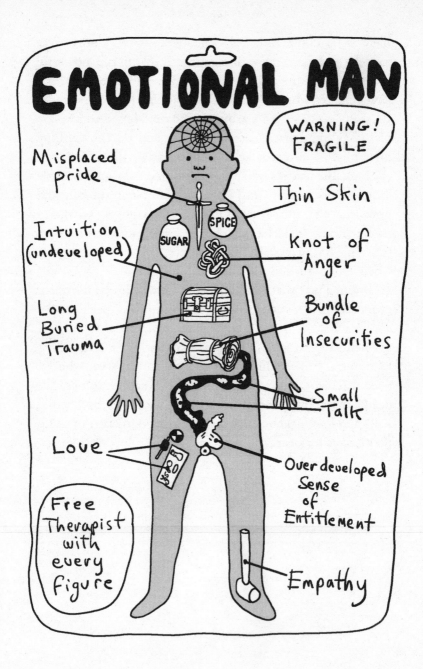

4

THE SHELL OF OBJECTIVITY

CALL ME NAIVE, BUT I BELIEVE ALL HUMANS ARE born good. Goodness is surely evolutionary: we want the human race to survive and the best way to do it is together. Evil is the behaviour of people who have been really fucked up.

Gender runs deep, but another aspect of our identity runs deeper: our personhood, our membership of the human race.

I also believe that all humans are born with the same deck of emotions, males and females. I believe male and female brains are pretty much the same. We have very similar hardware, it's the software – the way we are wired by experience – that is different. Males have the potential to be just as soppy and soft, tender and sweet, as females, it's just that males build up this brittle crust that masks and contains those feelings. They are encouraged to build up this crust from birth.

What are little boys made of?
What are little boys made of?
  Snips and snails
  And puppy dogs' tails
That's what little boys are made of

What are little girls made of?
What are little girls made of?
   Sugar and spice
   And all things nice
That's what little girls are made of

Boys grow up steeped in a culture that says that their feelings are somehow different from girls'. Boys have fewer feelings and theirs are simpler than girls'; boys are more robust, they don't care about things so much. But this downplaying of their emotional complexity is, I think, the aspect of masculinity that we most urgently need to change. Men need to transform their relationship with violence, performance and power. That change must begin with their emotions, by allowing boys and men more emotional space. A positive change in masculinity would be a massive positive change for the world. Emotional illiteracy is difficult for boys to deal with, yet they are brought up to accept this as readily as their beards growing and voices breaking.

People seem to like the idea that gender is somehow deeply influenced by our genes, no matter how little scientific evidence there is that they play much of a role. There may be biological differences in male and female brains that shape women's ability to empathize, practise social cohesion, and avoid danger, all things that help in leaving more descendants; and in men cause a bias towards systems, a more rigidly organized view of the world and an attraction to taking risks. But these differences have a tiny effect on gender roles compared to conditioning. We love to think that boys are 'naturally' more physical, less well behaved, more stoic. I think we like the idea that gender is in our genes because it is convenient, it lets us off the hook. It lets parents off the hook for the gendered ways we treat our children, consciously or unconsciously. It lets society off the hook for how we encourage gender stereotypes, and it lets us all off the hook for acting them out every minute of every day. One thing humans have definitely genetically evolved to like is convenience.

People trying to refute the idea of conditioned gender always cite the fact that research shows gender differences as fairly consistent across all cultures. However, gender roles are *not* the same across all cultures. The idea of what makes male and female behaviour is pretty fluid, as anthropologist Margaret Mead found in three primitive societies in Papua New Guinea in 1935, and wrote about in her book *Sex and Temperament*. In one tribe, the Arapesh, both men and women were peaceful and did not make war, while in the Mundugumor tribe both men and women were warlike. Unsurprisingly, the child-rearing styles of each tribe reflected their temperaments, so handing down the love or the violence. Curiously the Mundugumor built very good huts while those of the Arapesh were quite slapdash. I have always thought perfectionism unlovable!

From birth, boys are taught to act like men, the gendered inflections in how society treats children gradually becoming more pronounced as the child grows, from 'oh, look at him kick, he's going to be a footballer when he grows up' to 'suck it up, be tough, boys don't cry'. At this point, the parents of Islington rise up as one and refute my claim. 'We bring up our boys as free, loving, tender, empathetic, gentle souls,' they say. I'm sure they do, and the young men in question are probably delightful, and a tiny privileged minority, and I'm pretty sure their mothers still do most of the childcare and housework or employ other women to do it.

We have a lot of work to do: tougher parts of the country and most of the rest of the world are producing old-school men. At this point, I ask those Islington parents if they would rather have a tomboy or a sissy and their gender-neutral parenting policy crumbles slightly. Would Dad rather walk down the high street with his six-year-old son in a tutu waving a pink fairy wand or with their daughter in dungarees waving a plastic sword? They give me a guilty look, as if to say, 'You're right, the male role is more heavily policed, even by us.' But it is an unfair, biased question. In our society, 'sissy' is a derogatory, humiliating term for a feminine boy, and 'tomboy', a term for a masculine girl, has overtones of rough-hewn cool. If I phrased the question as 'What would you rather have: a feminine boy or a masculine girl?' the response might be more even-handed. But I suspect the preference would be for neither. This is not wholly the parents wanting a nice, neatly gendered child, but also a fear that society is often unkind to children who do not fit into 'man' and 'woman' effortlessly.

Unless a young man's schooling in the ways of masculinity is very alternative, most boys hold a fairly cartoon vision of manhood in their psyches, their gender boiled down to cliché and symbol. Most boys will hopefully gain a more sophisticated and subtle understanding of how to be a man, but it takes courage to challenge group norms. It is an enlightened young man who notices his mates' sexist behaviour or is aware of a wider emotional vocabulary, let alone talks about it in the group. In my experience, all-male company can all too easily descend into bonds of the lowest common denominator.

Out of curiosity I went to a school reunion a few years ago. I met up with a couple of dozen classmates I had not

seen in thirty-five years. Most of the faces looked familiar, and when names were exchanged I could put stories to some of them. What struck me most was their responses to me. They had all followed my very public career over the last ten years with interest, but not one of them could tell me a single thing about how I was at school. Even a terse character description was beyond them. I had been a cypher. I had closed down. I had been numb.

I think I went through most of my boyhood and youth numb. Numb to the fear and anxiety I felt at home. It is a survival mechanism, an emotional bunker. When we numb ourselves like that, we don't just numb the bad stuff, we numb all the emotions. It's a crude remedy. I once employed an electrician to work on my house who would arrive at 6 a.m. 'Why do you start so early?' I asked. 'To avoid all those angry road-ragers,' he replied – angrily. We may try to numb anger, but when we do we numb joy and pleasure in the world too. This numbing does not mean we stop having the feelings, it just stops us from being aware that we are having them. Those feelings are still churning away, tensing our bodies, writing unconscious scripts for us, storing up stuff to unload on to the world, on to our kids, but preferably on to our therapists. This numbness also inhibits the ability to have good relationships as well, hence the low impact I had on my classmates.

When I take myself back to that place of retreat, I imagine it as a heightened version of masculinity, as if I were a wary warrior cutting himself off from the world in preparation for battle. This was my retreat to the bedroom, into fantasy. Real flesh-and-blood humans were too frightening and unpredictable. Girls were unbelievably desirable but also frightening. I think all men have this instinct to retreat into oneself to a greater or lesser degree. It is the self-sufficient hero but also the lonely suicide.

I take risks. I am very competitive. I love throwing myself and my bike at speed down bumpy, muddy hillsides, yet when I return I am filled with anxiety about confronting my next-door neighbour about his infuriatingly yappy dog. I encourage students to design dresses for me that make me look daft and attention-seeking, but I burn with shame for an age after a bad review of my work. Qualities that I might easily assign to masculinity are often inconsistent: physical bravery does not translate into social courage; confidence to dress how I desire does not extend to confidence about what I make.

Boys are taught to be brave but in quite a specific way, mainly when facing physical danger on the sports field or the playground. But what about emotional danger? When asking a girl out on a date, having that tricky conversation with a colleague or revealing some very personal information to a friend, all the bluster and machismo that is so easy when climbing a tree or tackling a bigger player is of no use. The skill set of a typical boy can let him down when he is given a chance to grow emotionally. Bluff boys often muddle through: they invariably 'work things out' between themselves by avoiding the issue, capitulating through fear of conflict. Boys are not brought up to be sensitive to their own feelings, so how are they meant to voice them in a disagreement or declaration of affection?

As a twelve-year-old I was once struggling to assemble a model aeroplane. My frustration somehow manifested itself as a vow to leave home, and I cycled off towards Chelmsford, ten miles away, where my extended family lived. Leaving home may have been the nuclear option, but it was the only one of which I was aware. Unconsciously I probably knew that I would meet my mother coming in the opposite direction, driving home from work. I think what I was really trying to say was 'I need a father to help me out with such things', but I never did.

Often these situations are blown out of proportion because they are not within a boy's comfort zone. They are situations that contain potential embarrassment and rejection, and they can't be resolved by our charging into them. We need to practise them, make mistakes, start with small steps, just like with physical skills, but boys are rarely taught these things early enough. Often boys are actively taught *not* to practise unmanly emotions. So they avoid them. Boys deprived of emotional succour from open relationships with parents, girls or each other seek other ways to gain self-esteem: they form hierarchies. This need to establish a pecking order is exacerbated by the fact that boys tend to socialize in larger, less intimate groups. This linking of self-worth to status has pervaded the whole business of being a man. To feel better about themselves, boys have to feel better than others.

The way in which boys generally avoid emotional expression can manifest itself in their exam choices. Laura McInerney, a journalist and former teacher, has written in the *Guardian* that although the big story is usually that too few girls are studying maths and physics, a more extreme gender imbalance exists in the arts and social sciences. Only 29 per cent of A-level English students are male, while 60 per cent of pupils taking A-level sociology and psychology are female. Despite men still dominating the arts at the top end, heading cultural institutions, directing movies, their work getting huge auction prices, most of those starting a career in the arts are women. Girls make up 90 per cent of performing-arts students. At the University of the Arts London, where I am Chancellor, 70 per cent of its nearly 18,000 students studying mainly visual art are female. As well as being brought up as potential breadwinners, boys are conditioned to be poorer communicators and less in touch with their emotional bodies, hence they think the arts are not for them.

Men buy into the idea that they are emotionally uncomplicated. They often prefer to find refuge in predictable lists and diagrams. They would rather take an engine to pieces than examine the messy interior of their own minds. We find comfort in the precision fit of part A into part B.

I visited a men's cree (Geordie for shed), where men who are lonely or having emotional difficulties can meet and share. The Men's Sheds movement, which started in Australia, is a brilliantly simple idea that helps to prevent men from feeling isolated. Men often feel they should be self-sufficient, and don't seek out social contact for its own sake, especially as they get older. A man's inability to reach out emotionally comes home to roost if he is widowed or gets divorced late in life. The Men's Shed movement capitalizes on the idea that men often find it easier to talk about personal things while they are doing something practical, as it distracts them from the fact that they might be 'opening up'. Give them a problem to fix, and before you know it the banter is flowing, says one group leader. So they do arts and crafts, or go on visits to such places as historic railways or museums of industrial heritage, and the problems come out sideways while they are ostensibly doing something. One young man said that he had got to a state where he had been unable to make eye contact or interact at even the most basic level of please and thank you. So afraid of intimacy had he become that he could not handle even that kind of rudimentary human interaction.

An online version of the Men's Sheds movement could be the PistonHeads website. Although it's ostensibly a site about cars, buried among the threads on body kits and winter tyre choices are surprisingly touching discussions on parenting, relationships and mental health. A quick scan brings up a thread on dealing with stubborn elderly fathers who resist moves to improve their care, one on how to make friends when moving to a new area, and talk of friends stuck in self-destructive behavioural cycles. Men can and will talk about tricky emotional subjects, but perhaps need the cover of a manly context and maybe anonymity to do it with ease.

This mirrors my own experience. Since the 1980s I have frequented a tea hut in Epping Forest, north-east of London. It is a gathering place for motorcyclists, cyclists and locals, and is a kind of non-alcoholic open-air pub. Once I was chatting to a middle-aged biker who had never visited the hut before. After listening to the general chat among our group for a while, he declared, with a twinkle, 'Oh, I get it, we can talk about anything up here as long as it is about motorcycling.' And he was right: what he meant was motorcycles were the pretext for covert intimacy. Conversations may start with an admiring remark about someone's machine, but could easily segue into something more emotional. The feelings might be revealed in innocuous talk of man and machine or might be more specifically personal. One man, a father of four girls under twelve, told of how he had wanted to sell up and move to France and how, in a French estate agent's, he had turned to his children to ask their opinion on a house and they all just burst into tears. At that point he said he sensed that leaving Essex wasn't an option. A sweet story of taking his children's feelings seriously, and I think you would find the equivalent of this among any specialist interest group, whether it be model railways, birdwatching or *Star Wars*.

With age and experience, I have learned that one does not die of embarrassment or shame, that it is OK to be wrong, to fail, to be rejected, to show weakness. In fact these are all extremely useful and often endearing things to talk about. To sit back in that chair marked 'I don't know, I'll take a punt, but maybe you are right' is very comfy. The way some men defend a trivial argument, one would think it was a matter of life and death. That to be wrong was to face annihilation.

Brené Brown, a research professor in social work, gave a remarkable TED talk called 'The Power of Vulnerability'. Just google 'vulnerability' and she's on the first page. Brown found that the people who had the best, most fulfilling relationships were those who took emotional risks and showed their weaknesses and failures, their vulnerable underbellies. They allow a way in for other people. She thinks that many people feel shame, which she understands as a fear of disconnection, a fear that says 'I'm not good enough', something that people are very reluctant to talk about. She thinks that the only difference between those of us who have a good sense of connection with others, and those who don't, is that the first group feel they are worthy of friendship and love. These people have the courage to show all of themselves, to lay out their stall, warts and all. To make good connections with others we need to be authentic, we need to understand our emotions and behave in a way that reflects those feelings. Sometimes those feelings may show us to fall short of a standard we hold in our heads. All too often we act how we feel we *should* be. We might be pleasantly surprised if we ignored that impulse and told it like it is.

Every so often in a bar I notice a man – often all muscles, or joshing with a raucous group of mates – who seems to have an unnamed fear in his eyes and a nervous laugh. He seems to be showing fear and discomfort at where he has found himself, as if he is trapped, playing out a role that does not fit. This man emits anxiety, as though for a brief moment he has managed to glimpse round the edge of the mask and realized that all the investment he has made in 'being a man' is suddenly worth nothing. All the laughing at offensive jokes, all the pumping iron, all the drinking, competing, all the suppressed pain and hiding of sadness, all the colluding in sexist office politics, all the coping alone, all the diseases diagnosed too late, all the hours of boredom talking about sport, all of it, all of it, all of it – for what? To keep up the act – to be a foot soldier for an imaginary leader that sits in the top corner office of our unconscious. That imaginary man is of course the CEO of the Department of Masculinity. This idealized self, this boss, is hegemonic masculinity (from the Greek *hegemon*, meaning 'leader'), the archetypal bully all men carry around in their heads, tutting, sighing and sniping when they don't come up to scratch.

To change our ideas and feelings about masculinity, we need someone to walk into the leader's office and question his authority. He will bluster and say we are mad, but he needs to be confronted.

Psychologist Carl Rogers used the word 'congruence' when describing this relationship between the idealized self and the real self. Congruence is when the two selves fit harmoniously, when a person's idealized self is congruent with their actual behaviour. However, the idealized self is an often unreachable version of ourselves that we and society create, while the real self is the messy, imperfect inner truth. We want to be the idealized version because we believe that society will then regard us positively, so we struggle to maintain a version that does not really fit. Rogers called this incongruence.

This has deep resonances around masculinity, because echoing darkly inside us is this archetypal man who not only does not fit us very well but also doesn't want us to talk about it. This idealized man is very brittle. He is so fragile that a casual rejection or slight can cause him to shatter and collapse. A survey of secondary-school boys found that their biggest fear was being ridiculed. The confining role that masculinity encourages means there are men out there fit to burst. They are loaded with shame because they feel they are inadequate, and being masculine they can't talk about it. The single biggest cause of death for men under the age of forty-five in the UK is suicide. Globally about twice as many men kill themselves as women, in developed countries it is three times as many, and in some Eastern European states men are six times as likely as women to kill themselves. For many, masculinity is a fatal burden. These figures are but the tip of an iceberg of lonely, depressed men who feel unable to reach out for meaningful human contact. We need to shout from the rooftops that masculinity is whatever you want it to be. That achieving successful traditional masculinity is like learning to be good at woodwork. For some guys it is really essential, for others it is fairly handy, but really it is not vital – it is simply an option.

When I am talking to men and want to explain the role of vulnerability in our relationships, I use the metaphor of the contact patch. When we are on two wheels, whether riding a motorcycle or a bicycle, our lives often depend on two tiny ellipses of rubber, the contact patches. The contact patch is the part of the tyre that is in contact with the road at any one time. Within limits the softer the rubber or the lower the tyre pressure, the more the tyre deforms and the larger the contact patch tends to be, and the more grip it affords. In a relationship, being more vulnerable means that more of you is in play and you are more prepared to be impacted upon by the other person. In relationships, just as on a motorcycle, our well-being depends on that contact patch. I can't emphasize the importance of vulnerability enough. It is central to men's future happiness. We need to rebrand vulnerability and emotion. A vulnerable man is not some weird anomaly. He is open to being hurt, but also open to love. This is emotional health. A man who does not bottle up anger, fear or sadness also experiences more joy and more intimate relationships.

The belief that self-sufficiency is a central plank of manliness can be so deeply held that it becomes a life or death issue. Vulnerability can seem such a terrible option that suicide is preferable. Simon Binner, who suffered from motor neurone disease, was the subject of Rowan Deacon's beautiful documentary *A Time to Die: Simon's Choice*. Several times in the film, as the disease progressively robs Simon of the power to speak, then to walk, Simon writes that the worst aspect of it was the humiliation, the unmanliness of it all, and that he would rather die. This was a funny, super-articulate, Oxbridge-educated man, yet he could not bear to be unmanned, to lose his independence.

Men are conditioned to deal with stress alone. This emotional self-sufficiency is ingrained early. Much more often than girls, boys ban their mothers from accompanying them to the school gate, and tell them to wait for them round the corner in the afternoon, because the pressure to act 'grown up' is so intense. Mothers skulk out of sight, a cuddly reminder of the feminized domestic sphere that boys are being programmed to escape from. We are reminded by every adventure film that a man is out there doing stuff in the world, acting in the public sphere. This is a situation that other, supposedly more primitive societies have ritualized in coming-of-age ceremonies that involve going into the wilderness or moving to the men's hut. I am not recommending that the wayward sons of middle England start jumping off towers with vines tied to their feet like the Vanuatu land divers, but I sometimes think that we would benefit enormously if we had in place some ritual programme to channel all that chaotically unfocused male feeling. A war perhaps? I jest . . . just.

I am not alone in thinking that some kind of ritualized passage to manhood would benefit boys today. Many of the examples I have found from around the world involve going off into the wild and experiencing some difficult or painful trial. These may work, but I can't help feeling that we need a version that prepares young men for modern, urban, gender-equal society. At the core of any ritual there needs to be an examination and celebration of emotion in all its richness. Being able to withstand the pain of wearing a glove filled with vicious stinging bullet ants for ten minutes without showing distress, as the Sateré-Mawé tribe of the Amazon do in an initiation rite, is not preparing the contemporary male for the world of Tinder, house husbands and a service economy.

Many old-school men, in their far from blissful ignorance, don't seem to be aware of the harm that maintaining an outdated emotional numbness is doing, not least to their relationship chances. Women are marrying at a much later age these days, and are spending more quality time with female friends. They are learning the value of true intimacy and support, and are better able to see what a healthy relationship can offer. The result is that the bar is set higher for the marriageable man, and being single for a man is not healthy, no matter what some men's rights groups like MGTOW think. Married men live longer on average than single men. The companionship and emotional support offered by a partner have significant effects on a man's well-being. There is no reason to believe that this is not true in gay marriage as well. Men are more reliant on their partners than women are. A partner can be the one who keeps an eye on the health of a man's mind and body, as he may be incapable of noticing or acknowledging it himself.

This emotional illiteracy is not like poor education, some blight on the lower orders. Numbness to feelings may be even worse in the politely repressed middle classes. My father-in-law, Mark, was a company chairman, an army officer in the Second World War and a member of a golf club, a truly old-school man. When he was old and alone, my wife would ask him how he was feeling and he would always reply with a brusque 'fine'. A lifetime of being in charge and performing traditional masculinity meant he was almost incapable of any other answer. She found a more reliable method of ascertaining his mood or health was to ask after his boon companion, the dog. He would project his feelings on to the dog, and in this way my wife was able to get a rough reading of his state of mind and body.

Footage of UN spokesman Chris Gunness breaking down in tears as he spoke of the horrors occurring in Gaza

went viral. It was newsworthy because such spokespeople and reporters are supposed to be dispassionate and impartial. To show such feelings was thought by many to be 'unprofessional'. And lo, the inherited mental health issues of the old-school man are cast as a necessity for serious employment.

Old-school man should be made aware of the costs and increasing obsolescence of maintaining a stiff upper lip. This habit of denying, recasting or suppressing emotion may give him the veneer of 'professionalism', but as David Hume put it, 'Reason is a slave to the passions.' To be unaware or unwilling to examine feelings means that those feelings have free rein to influence behaviour unconsciously. Unchecked, they can motivate a man covertly, unacknowledged, often wreaking havoc. Even if they are rooted in long-past events in the deep unconscious, these emotions still exist, churning in the dark at the bottom of the well.

Being male, middle class, and from a generation who still valued the stiff upper lip, our old-school man is an ideal candidate for low emotional awareness, sitting as he does in a gender/class/age nexus marked 'Unexploded Emotional Time Bomb'. Emotion is a physical thing. We hold it in every cell of our bodies, it is present in how we sit and stand, and some skilled therapists can read whole emotional histories in a client before they even open their mouths, using their client's body language as a guide. Sometimes I have the feeling that men see their bodies as a liability, corruptible, full of messy feelings, when all they want is a vehicle to transport the magnificent head of state, their brain. Men may know how to maintain their bodies like a machine with healthy diet and exercise, but they may be unaware of or ignore the symptoms of emotional malady. One way to maintain good emotional health is through regular intimate contact with friends.

Despite all the ads full of beery cheerleading around buddies and bromance, men are generally not so good at maintaining friendships as women. Male friends are often made in specific contexts such as school, shared houses, work, hobbies and sports, and if the context changes the friends drop off the radar too. Men tend not to prioritize relationships, unlike their work or their physical fitness. The emotional richness of a relationship is often left unacknowledged, as many men are less aware of their feelings.

I remember realizing in my mid thirties that I had no close male friends. I was married with a young daughter who took up all my time when I was not working on my solitary labours. I sought out male friendship through motorcycling and mountain biking, but it was difficult to find someone with whom I wanted to spend time when we were not doing our shared hobby. It was a bit like finding a girlfriend: it took a while to find someone not just with shared interests but who was emotionally open and funny as well and lived fairly close by. Geography is often overlooked in the search for community in the Internet age, but friendships are much harder to maintain over long distances. I think one of the reasons a man might not register the importance of good platonic relationships is that they don't involve that primal driver, sex.

Men, bless 'em, are tethered to a monster, a demon conjoined twin, a one-man 'wrong crowd' who will often drag them into bad behaviour. The penis is at once us and not of us. In puberty, particularly, it seems to have a life of its own, jutting out at embarrassing angles at the slightest provocation. I remember more than once having to leave the bus carrying my Adidas sports bag over my groin as the vibration of the engine and the presence of a female, any female, had been more than enough entertainment for my unruly mole rat.

For many men, sex boils and ferments just below the surface of a crust of civility. The comedian Phill Jupitus describes masturbation as the 'male screen saver'. If a man is not concentrating on something, his brain goes into sleep mode and sex swims into his awareness. Instead of a view of Yosemite Valley or a swirling universe, a back catalogue of diary porn shuffles across his mind screen, and the desire to jerk off takes over.

Men, particularly when young, view the world through a head-up display of sexual desire. A head-up display is when the dashboard dials are projected on to the windscreen so that a driver does not have to look down to read them, he kind of looks *through* them at the view ahead. A man's view of the world is always compromised by feedback from the engine of sex thrumming away in their pants. It becomes apparent how strong this influence of sexual desire is after an orgasm. For a few brief minutes the fog of lust drifts away and a kind of exotic clarity, a hint of objectivity, hoves into view. My wife once asked what I was thinking of in my post-coital reverie. I sought a metaphor for the style of thoughts running through my brain: 'Mending watches,' I replied.

I have talked before about how I notice that a strong component of masculinity is nostalgia. One aspect of all of us, both men and women, that seems to me to be permanently looking back is our sexuality. It may feel like our sex drive is always on the hunt, but what it is hunting for, I think, is in the past. Our sexualities are, on the whole, shaped by our childhoods. Or rather they are dressed, directed and scripted by our childhoods. Biological imperatives may be at the centre of our sex drive, but the emotions that get attached to it, the power plays and dramatic roles we act out in our sex lives, we learn as children. We may be genetically predisposed to be straight or gay, identify as a male or a female or in between, but I think the attitudes, cues, contexts, power relationships, props and costumes are supplied by conditioning. And our closest relationships when we are growing up are, of course, with our family, who in turn reflect to a greater or lesser degree the relationship styles of their society and era. The scripts of our sexual fantasies are usually roughed out by our experiences as children. The central characters may be played by someone from your office or off the telly, but the dynamic, the relationship styles, the story arc, all have an older origin.

I don't think there is necessarily an exact correlation between *certain* childhood experiences and *certain* sexualities. I think it might be more like a treasure hunt than a recipe. One goes through one's early years collecting experiences, influences and traumas, and at puberty one cashes them in at a counter marked sexual preferences and one is handed back an identity card or licence that pretty much fixes one's sexuality. This can be an unconscious process, of course, and one may not realize what is written on one's licence until confronted with an arousing situation years later. I knew I was kinky from a very young age, maybe at seven, I just didn't know how to describe it. I read about transvestites in a Sunday tabloid when I was about thirteen. This was when I first read what was already written on my licence. At last I had words for it; on reading about other people who felt like me, the compulsion to dress up was suddenly no longer just a secret internal dialogue, it was no longer just something I communicated between my conscious and unconscious. Now I saw there was a way of telling the world, or not.

So the liberal, politically correct, modern metrosexual may to his horror find that the delicate little creature lying limply between his legs takes an unhealthy interest in out-dated gender relationships. Mr Peepee, the demon sibling, may like subservient women wearing high heels, yet his twin finds himself choosing to live in a group who all agree on gender equality and where all the girls wear trainers. Several times I have asked audiences to put up their hand if they have sexual fantasies where the central theme is gender equality. No one ever raises their hand. (Who would? Nick Clegg maybe?) Perhaps it is a silly request, or maybe they are all dreaming of being bent over the desk by the boss, or being the boss. No one gets aroused by thinking about holding hands in matching fleeces while shopping for sofas or sharing childcare, do they? Often the difficulties we face in relationships with partners is a mismatch between the power relationships that turn us on sexually and the ones that work on a day-to-day emotional basis. Men tend to prioritize the sex component more when choosing a part-ner, and women tend to prioritize the day-to-day emotional relationship. This is exemplified by the phenomenon of lesbian bed death, where lesbians' sex lives dry up because they choose a partner who is just like them and that does not result in a sexy power imbalance. Men usually prioritize sex. A gay friend told me that when dating he used to instinc-tively inject a power imbalance into the relationship to make it sexier. If he thought his boyfriend was posh, my friend said he lived in Kilburn (then a poor area); if he thought the boyfriend was working class, he said he lived in West Hampstead (a posh area). He actually lived an equal distance between the two Tube stations.

Difference and an imbalance of power are big components of what turns us all on, not just the kinky ones. My wife and many other psychotherapists and psychologists say we are all fetishists, it's just that some fetishes (slim, big-breasted women; tall, muscular men) are accepted as 'normal' while others (rubber, bondage, spanking) are 'kinky' and some (children and corpses) are illegal. It is in the area of fetishism where I have noted this tendency for sexual nostalgia most clearly, maybe because it is dealing with objects linked by style or use to earlier periods. Transvestites often dress in styles reminiscent of their mother's generation – not by mistake, but because their sexuality has led them to choose more mature styles, maybe because they are associated partly with old-fashioned gender power relationships. Adult babies choose to wear terry towelling or disposable nappies depending on when they were brought up. Girdles, shampoo and sets, mackintoshes, petticoats, gym slips, leg braces and straitjackets, all fetishes, are all from another era.

People from across the sexual spectrum find adrenaline a strong aphrodisiac. The excitement of taking risks, coupled with sex, is a potent cocktail. For the kinky, the risk might be death from asphyxiation, public humiliation or criminal conviction; for more vanilla types, the risk is the wife finding out.

Ritualistic BDSM fetishes are often described as the sexualized replay of childhood trauma. Beatings or humiliations experienced when young are reframed unconsciously as erotic excitements in adulthood. If we are all fetishists, maybe 'normal' human relationships are just as backward-looking. My wife says she does not believe in love at first sight, only transference at first sight – transference being the transferring of emotional response from a past relationship on to a new one, often because the new person reminds you physically of the previous figure, very commonly a parent or previous lover. Transference is usually unconscious.

I once took a violent dislike to a young man in group therapy, and made up all sorts of reasons for it over several months. It was only when I talked to my therapist about it that I realized this fellow was the same age and had the same appearance as my stepfather when he moved in. He even had the same habit of cracking his knuckles. The minute I realized it was all transference, my antipathy towards the man dissolved. I wonder how many relationships dissolve when the transference wears off?

What I think I am hinting at here is that the big investment many men have in maintaining old-fashioned gender power relationships could be sexual. What turns them on is socially and politically out of date. There is a lag between developments in society and the unconscious forces that shape our sexualities. And it is not just men. The writer Lori Gottlieb, in a *Guardian* article entitled 'Does Equality Kill Sex?', cites a study which appeared in *American Sociological Review* called 'Egalitarianism, Housework and Sexual Frequency in Marriage'. The study surprised many with its finding that in couples where the man did many of the chores that are considered to be feminine – ironing, cooking and vacuuming, for example – they reported less frequent and less satisfying sex. Housework does not make a man sexier. Esther Perel, a couples therapist, puts it bluntly: 'Most of us are turned on at night by the very things that we'll protest about during the day.' When I talked to a women's therapy group, several members bemoaned the lack of real 'manly' men in middle-class circles these days. But when I quizzed them about this, they admitted that they only wanted him in the bedroom department; the rest of the time they wanted a nice sensitive chap who would clean out the cat litter without being asked. Good luck with that. Curiously, the increasing number of women voicing submissive fantasies (see, for example, sales figures of *Fifty Shades of Grey*) may be related to increasing gender equality. Subservience is now more a sexy leisure option than an enforced role.

So changing social contexts can affect our sexuality. I think the opposite can also be true. Sexuality can influence our general behaviour, particularly men's, in profound ways, especially if you throw in a heavy dose of adrenaline sparked by violence or risk. The Department of Masculinity knows that the man with status in society also has a better chance of more sex. Churning away, deep in the unconscious, our sexuality drives forward certain behaviours and choices that it thinks will increase the chances of an arousing encounter. Power at its most primal leads to the biggest choice of sexual partners. Violent warlords take it for granted. Many a rock star, politician or celebrity sportsman has 'somehow found himself' in the position where women throw themselves at him.

Male sexuality these days is commonly portrayed as dangerous and retrograde. All men are potential rapists/ abusers, some say; our penises are stuck in the dark ages, we want a harem. Adding to men's confusion about these things are advances in fertility science, which may lead to male sexuality as a sperm delivery system becoming redundant. Men today are confronted by a rapidly shifting gender minefield. They can no longer trust Mr Todger as a reliable compass to guide them through. The gender landscape is also one of myths, one of which is that every guy thinks every other guy is having great sex three times a day, or at least three times a week. Men grow up thinking that to be real men they need to have sex almost as often as they think about it. A psychotherapist who works with mainly middle-aged men has told me that he thinks less than 5 per cent of his clients are getting regular sex, and these are not losers in broken relationships but regular married guys.

Other myths are promoted by online porn. Many younger men now grow up absorbing the myth that normal sex is hours of pumping, high-intensity intercourse with shaven supermodels. Imagine their distress when confronted with a real woman, whose company they enjoy, and it turns out she has pubic hair. Or when the initial lust wears off and they start to feel unlucky and duped. Well, sorry, fellas, that might well be normal: we have to work at relationships. The gulf between increasingly pornified expectations of what sex should be like and the experience of real, day-to-day co-habiting is something that many young men find hard to deal with. Accustomed to a diet of porn selected to match their sexual tastes perfectly, when they are confronted with emotionally complex interactions with real women that (gasp) have their own agenda, it can just be too much.

One of the cultural phenomena that have come out of the digital age is what Japanese author Maki Fukasawa termed 'herbivore men', or 'grass-eater men'; in other words, men who express no interest in getting married or finding a girlfriend. In 2010 over half of Japanese men in their twenties and thirties declared themselves herbivores. This

may be a very specifically Japanese phenomenon to do with
the nation's history after the Second World War and with a
culture with an unhealthy relationship to shame. But the
Internet is everywhere. Many men might well feel that mas-
turbating along to endlessly varied pornography is preferable
to embarking on emotionally exposing, embarrassing relationships with flesh-and-blood women. Herbivore men
might be canaries in the coalmine, warning of needed change
in the way we bring up boys. The appalling ubiquity of online
sexist and racist abuse speaks of lonely, angry men. If we
don't teach them emotional literacy, they might well end up
living lonely, unhealthy, shorter lives.

A sign of impending change may be the increasing occurrence of the male who performs traditional masculinity
inadequately. The doofus, the klutz, the geek, the nerd,
Homer Simpson, David Brent, any number of male comedic
personas. He wears a shortsleeve shirt and tie or a sweater
knitted by his aunt. He may just be inadequately masculine,
or he may just not care, or he may just be resistant to the
pressure to perform manliness. The doofus is a figure of
fun. How we laugh as a thousand generations of male pride
is trashed. How we laugh when young men are left looking
in the waste bin of history for the remnants of a meaningful
role for the psyche they have inherited. How we laugh when
they fail to get the girl, the job or the joke. But maybe we
should have more compassion for them, because how we
will scream when the boil of their thwarted masculinity
bursts and they come back armed with an assault rifle and
start firing randomly.

These comic doofus characters may play a role in testing
the boundaries of masculinity, softening up the audience
for change. They may also be a sop to those young men who

sense that the role of the traditionally manly man may be not only too difficult, but impossible in the current social context, so frowned upon is it by young women enthusiastically taking on board fourth-wave feminism. One thing I know is that they are not going to satisfy boys looking for a hero to emulate.

Progressive men are confused. They want to do the right thing but feel everything they do is tainted by millennia of bad male behaviour. My generation of men often feel that they have to continually apologize for our fellow males and walk round with a metaphorical notice round our necks saying 'I'm not a rapist'. More than once I have had conversations with men about the embarrassing manoeuvring they do to avoid making lone women fearful when walking down dark streets, such as hanging back or changing their route. 'I'm not a rapist, honest!'

Masculinity is not a condition in isolation. The Department of Masculinity has a hand in everything. If we manage to reframe a version of masculinity fit for a happy future then perhaps we would be less likely to go to war, more empathetic to the weak, less bound up in the status of wealth and more concerned about the rewards of good relationships. This would be great. We can talk about masculinity until we are blue in the face, but if the world's other huge problems are not confronted, the unhelpful versions of what it is to be a man will surely thrive. Masculinity will not change unless the economic, cultural and social conditions welcome that change.

I increasingly wonder if the problem of such discussions is the masculine demand for certainty. Men might want a summation and an exact recipe for ideal future masculinity, but the future of men needs to be mapped out in the process as much as the content.

How we talk about masculinity might be just as important, if not more so, than *what* we say. The very idea that there is a strict set of rules needs to be chucked away. The future of masculinity is a plethora of masculinities.

The 'ideal' future might just be increasing tolerance and celebration of a spectrum of masculinities born out of increasing awareness of what feels good for the individual and for society. Ongoing, pluralistic, messy negotiation may be the best I can offer you, but it is a damn sight better than the suicidal rigidity of the cliché of masculinity held on to by so many.

We men need to stop thinking of masculinity as immutable, even within our own lifetimes. One thing therapy has taught me is that you can change how you feel about things, even deep fundamental things. It just takes motivation, education and a good bit of time. Men can learn how not to fear the alternatives, to realize that no one dies of embarrassment.

We need to stop dismissing men as cardboard, brittle, inflexible, unable to change. After all, they have pretty much the same brains as women. I think the problem is that the male *role* at the present time is very constrictive. Men are very good at unconsciously policing it all the time. Vital to healthy change is a tolerance of difference. Men need to stop giving other men, and themselves, a hard time for not attaining the standards of masculinity. This will be tricky: men like an instruction manual, but one hasn't been written for the future of manhood yet. Old-school masculinity has a long history and a nice clear set of rules. The future alternative is vaguer, more contingent; as in all exploration, we don't quite know where we are going. It has few heroes and narratives. This new flexible man will have to adapt not only to a new gender role but to a version that works in different cultures, classes, ethnicities and religions.

These changes will need to work in emotional time as opposed to intellectual time. We can understand logically the benefits of a new situation quite quickly, but our emotions, so embedded in our bodies and unconscious, can take generations to change. Something as woven into our beings as gender probably takes centuries to truly transform, but we can help speed it up. If the environment in which our gendered human is living is changed, then the nature of gender itself will have to adapt in order to thrive. Positive discrimination is a controversial solution. I believe it is very necessary. If we force change towards a gender-equal society, then the male role will have to adapt to fit in with it. We can see it happening already in places like the boardroom. Companies are being forced to take on a certain proportion of women; men will see and enjoy the benefits or, if they insist on being old-fashioned, they will suffer for not adapting.

But, of course, this nuanced, variable masculinity might suffer next to the fixed, totemic nature of the old. Someone once said that maturity is being able to hold two contradictory messages in your head at the same time. With adolescence these days seeming to stretch to thirty-five, maturity is a hard sell. We need to firm up what it *is* to be a man in the twenty-first century, because other retrograde forces are happy to promote a seductive, familiar, easy-to-assemble package.

An emergent masculinity may be one that prizes tolerance, flexibility, plurality and emotional literacy in the same way that strength, certainty and stoicism have been celebrated in the past. Give boys a finishing line and maybe they will race to cross it.

Perhaps we need to first bury and mourn the old-school man with all due dignity and ceremony. In 2015 I attended the Durham Miners' Gala, and I think it gave me a taste of what that ceremony might look like. The Gala was traditionally the day when coalminers would come into the city to sign on for another year's work. Now it is a festival celebrating a nearly extinct culture of heavy industry and a rally for left-wing feeling. From all over the country, groups gather to parade the trade union banners of the now mainly defunct pits. With the weight of history, the crowds and the brass bands playing, it is a joyous and moving sight. The emotional peak is to be found in the blessing of the banners. New banners, nowadays often made for schools or community groups rather than the pits, are paraded down the aisle of Durham's magnificent cathedral, accompanied by mournful brass band music. To me, this poignant ceremony felt like the funeral for a sort of man, that stoic provider who worked down the mines, and perhaps it is time to move on.

I am not suggesting that we should say goodbye to everything that old-school men stood for. When I asked Jerry Hyde, a psychotherapist, what masculinity is, his unhesitating response was 'tenderness'. A curious answer perhaps, but gentle men do possess a quality of tenderness that is very masculine. A gentle man is a powerful person who has the strength to crush something, physically or emotionally, yet chooses not to, chooses love and tenderness. Masculine tenderness has a straightforwardness, perhaps as a result of the conditioning that 'boys are simple creatures'. Masculine compassion is a calm, dependable arm round the shoulder. Good men are 'rocks', invested with introverted qualities that are not celebrated enough. These qualities are often sidelined by the melodramatic bluster of cartoon masculinity.

In many communities a major issue is a lack of good modern male role models at every level. Many boys grow up fatherless, and few teachers in nursery and primary schools are male, so kids look to the media, where there is a back catalogue of brilliant old-school male role models: stoic, violent cowboys; stoic, violent superheroes; stoic, violent computer-game soldiers. Lovely, funny, creative men are out there, but they have their work cut out. I think Barack Obama presents a superb version of manhood. His calm thoughtfulness, emotional ease, wit and eloquence in the face of gross expectation and intractable problems is breathtaking. At a national level we have David Attenborough or Chris Packham, with their intense joy, curiosity and compassion for the natural world. I grew up with David Bowie, the patron saint of the boy in his bedroom who felt alienated by the male culture of his peers. Then there is reformed bad boy David Beckham offering to soothe a stranger's baby, carrying it up and down the aisle for a fellow passenger while she ate her meal on a plane.

I can't help thinking that in order to qualify as a modern, sharing, caring, male role model one might have to step partly out of the public eye and into the domestic sphere, so role models of an alternative masculinity might not be high-profile celebrities. Despite the fact that in 2012 only 35 per cent of British people declared themselves part of a traditional family set-up where dad is the breadwinner and mum is the carer, the change in male domestic behaviour is

Man friendly childcare

Creche Bar

Give your pre-verbal child a head start with

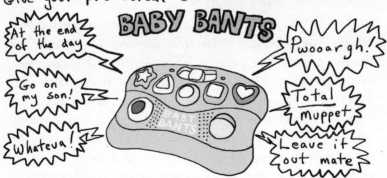

slow. Women still do two thirds of the childcare, and only a tiny proportion, less than 5 per cent, of men have taken up Shared Parental Leave when they become new fathers. Taking extended paternity leave, in other words more than a few weeks, is seen as detrimental to career progression by both employees and bosses. Many men do genuinely want to spend more time with their young families, and true gender equality won't happen until we all take their needs seriously. But whenever I read reports about the slow take-up of existing fathering opportunities, I sense that the subtext is that men know (though they whisper it) that looking after young children at home is bloody hard work and (even quieter whisper) pretty boring.

Stay-at-home dads and male gay parents are becoming more common and are great examples to all men. But men are still very good at making up seemingly rational but vague 'work' reasons to avoid childcare, or saying they 'have' to get their exercise time in 'or they will go mad'. Maybe we need to change not only the image of the stay-at-home dad but the practice. Perhaps we need new styles of childcare arrangements that appeal to fathers: stock car racing with child seats in the back? A category in marathons for dads with baby buggies? Pubs with crèches?

I think adaptability is the key to our masculine future. Masculinity is mainly a construct of conditioned feelings around people with penises. It can feel writ in stone, but emotions and feelings can be changed. I think that men need to look inside themselves (open the bonnet), become more aware of their feelings (read the manual) and start adapting (upgrade). A common refrain in the therapy world is 'act as if' – if you want to change your feelings, act as if they have, and lo and behold the new behaviour starts to feel familiar and, hopefully, better. At first men might perform a camp version of the future, where they self consciously play out an awkward vision of an alternative masculinity, as new styles of behaviour can often feel wrong, but men might be surprised at how quickly they feel right and, dare I say it, quite manly.